Japanese Baseball

and other stories

Japanese Baseball

and other stories

W.P. KINSELLA

THISTLEDOWN PRESS

Canadian Cataloguing in Publication Data

Kinsella, W.P.
Japanese baseball and other stories
ISBN 1-894345-18-5
1. Baseball stories, Canadian (English).*   I. Title.
PS8571.I57 J36 2000   C813'.54   C00-920205-6
PR9199.3.K443 J36 2000

Cover painting and design by Barbara Turner
Typeset by Thistledown Press Ltd.
Printed and bound in Canada

Thistledown Press Ltd.
633 Main Street
Saskatoon, Saskatchewan
S7H 0J8

Thistledown Press gratefully acknowledges the financial assistance of the
Canada Council for the Arts, the Saskatchewan Arts Board, and the
Government of Canada through the Book Publishing Industry Development
Program for its publishing program.

Contents

ACKNOWLEDGEMENTS

"Japanese Baseball" appeared in *Dandelion*, and *Iowa City Magazine*, and "Wavelengths" "The Arbiter" and "The Mansions of Federico Juarez" in *Iowa City Magazine*. "The First and Last Annual Six Towns Area Old-Timers' Game" was published as a collectors' edition chapbook by Coffee House Press of Minneapolis. "The Lime Tree" was published by *Elysian Fields Magazine*, and "Tulips" accepted by *Dugout Magazine*. "The Kowloon Cafe" was accepted by Heartlands. "The Indestructable Hadrian Wilks" was anthologized in *Baseball Fantastic* published by Quarry Press, and published by Passages North. "Fred Noonan Flying Services" was anthologized in *Baseball Fantastic*, and published by Westview.

Japanese Baseball
and other stories

The Kowloon Cafe

"You want to do what?" the general manager, Mike Peckinpaugh, said to me, after I suggested the baseball club hire a Feng Shui master to determine the exact site for the new baseball stadium.

"Understanding tradition is a key to doing business," I heard myself saying.

"What is this Fing Shing business anyway?" said Peckinpaugh, looking at me suspiciously. He is short and bald, built like a sack of potatoes with legs. Long ago, during World War II, he played twenty-eight games at second base for the St. Louis Browns.

I launched into a long explanation.

Because the Kowloon Cafe building sat at an odd angle to the street, everyone assumed that the ancient, bizarrely-shaped, three-story frame structure with gingerbread at its top corners, had been built before the street it stood next to had been created.

When I began to research the history of the Kowloon Cafe, I discovered that such was not the case.

Yes, that was the only explanation, people said, the Kowloon Cafe had been built before the angle of the street had been finalized. All the other buildings were parallel to the street, their fronts tight against the sidewalk, while the Kowloon Cafe building sat several feet back from the sidewalk, at an unnatural angle, the east side of the building withdrawn about four feet from the sidewalk, the west side about eight feet back.

Chen Wah, the man who'd built the Kowloon Cafe building, had emigrated from China as a young man. In America, in Ohio, he quickly became Charlie Wah, then just Charlie to all but his banker and his immediate family.

He never talked about why or how he'd emigrated.

"Long time ago," was all he said when asked.

"Did you work on the railroad when you were a young man?" a reporter once asked him.

"Work for railroad, yes," Charlie Wah said, but his eyes were focused somewhere over the reporter's shoulder, and his smile, while bright, gave no indication as to whether his statement was true, or whether he was giving an answer expected of him.

On his arrival in the United States, Charlie Wah worked for several years, first in the kitchen, then as a waiter, in a small restaurant in Columbus, Ohio, the owner of which had reportedly sponsored Charlie as an immigrant, claiming him to be a son, or nephew, or younger brother, which he may or may not have been.

In turn, Charlie Wah, a few months after the Kowloon

Cafe opened for business, sponsored the immigration of a wife and an almost-grown child.

Charlie's age was always a matter of speculation among his customers, for when he opened the Kowloon Cafe, he looked thirty-five, yet there was a tinge of gray in the prickly looking hair at his temples.

People surmised that he must have married very young, for it seemed impossible for him to be the father of the boy who arrived to live with him.

"Trip home, eighteen years ago," Charlie would say gently, when someone had the bad taste to inquire, and a lot of his customers displayed bad taste. "One month visit. Have always had wife. Have girl, too. She married now, stay in China."

In the years after the wife and son arrived, three daughters and another son were born to Charlie Wah and his wife.

Forty years later, when the Kowloon Cafe was to be torn down to make way for the new major league baseball stadium, Charlie Wah looked scarcely a year older than the day the cafe opened. His black hair was now iron-gray, otherwise he could have just stepped out of the framed photograph that hung behind the cash register, showing him on the day the cafe opened, standing in front of the restaurant, his staff gathered behind him, a banner, red lettering on white canvas, reading Grand Opening, floating in the front window.

Charlie Wah arrived in our city in 1938, and bought three lots in a developing business district on the edge of downtown. He hired an architect, a large German with a red face, suspenders bulging over a beer-induced corpulence, to design a three-story building that would run the full length of his property.

The Kowloon Cafe was to occupy the ground floor, while half the second story was to be for Charlie and his family.

The remainder of the second floor, and all of the third was to be rooms, some to be used by staff, the remainder to be rented to the public.

When the building was completed, the front windows glowed with flamingo-pink neon, announcing KOWLOON CAFE. Above the door was a small two-sided sign with the single word EAT in runny green neon on either side. There was a hand-lettered sign above a door on the right front of the building that read KOWLOON ROOMS, and under that Day, Week, Month.

There are still old-timers in the neighbourhood who remember *the argument*. For many of them, like Gephardt the locksmith, whose shop was directly across the street from Charlie Wah's three lots, it was the only time they'd ever seen Charlie Wah lose his temper.

The argument began because Charlie Wah insisted the Kowloon Cafe building be constructed at some exact angles he had predetermined, and not, as the architect had insisted, parallel to Ohio Avenue, like all the other buildings on both sides of the street.

The architect, snapping his suspenders, his large reddish mustache quivering like a vegetable brush, pointed out logically and with some authority, that if the Kowloon Cafe building was built parallel to Ohio Avenue, Charlie Wah need use only two of his three lots. The remaining lot could be sold, or held, or even covered with an additional building.

"In my country position is the essence of life," Charlie replied mildly. "The position of the building is vastly important to the success or failure of my business, to the happiness of myself and my family."

The architect snorted and said something rude.

Charlie Wah sighed, acknowledged that the changes he required might cause the architect some minor inconvenience.

The architect huffed and raged.

"I will have to change my drawings," he thundered. While continuing to make his point he lapsed into German on more than one occasion.

Charlie Wah remained firm. He stomped his feet in the dust, as the two men tromped up and down Ohio Avenue, and spoke loudly in Chinese, whapping two fingers of his right hand into the palm of his left to emphasize the points he was making.

The architect eventually gave in to Charlie's wishes, though he increased his fee by three hundred dollars, which Charlie paid, happy to have the specifications altered to meet his needs.

Now, over forty years later, the Kowloon Cafe is the only functioning building on the block. When it was first opened it immediately became *the* place to go for Chinese food in the city. The cafe was crowded at breakfast by workers from nearby factories, drinking from bottomless cups of coffee while ingesting pancakes, waffles, or French toast, accompanied by huge slices of ham or bacon. At lunch it was jammed again, sometimes with the same workers, more often with business people from the nearby downtown, clerks, stockbrokers, lawyers.

At dinner the clientele was mainly business people, though usually husbands and wives, or dating couples, for Charlie Wah's restaurant quickly became known for the best Chinese food in the city. The late night trade encompassed all walks of society, with the sleazier types remaining until the first workers began wandering in for breakfast. The doors of the Kowloon Cafe were never closed.

And Charlie Wah was always there, or at least seemed to be.

Behind the glass counter at the front of the cafe Charlie was always smiling, brandishing a fistful of menus, dressed in a tan restaurant jacket and black pants, pointing the way to a vacant table. He was always smiling as he collected cash, exchanging a joke with a departing customer, handing a green mint to a child. He was always smiling as he rented a room late at night to a transient, or to a couple, where the man signed the register, Mr. and Mrs. Smith.

"All Amelicans named Smith," Charlie would say, laughing, looking over the dog-eared book in which his renters registered.

"Always take cash myself," Charlie often said to customers. And it was true. There never seemed to be a time when Charlie was not on the cash register. "Cook may take home a couple of chicken wings if I'm not in kitchen, but I never lose cash if I'm handle register myself."

Before the foundations for the Kowloon Cafe building were begun Charlie Wah brought in a Feng Shui master from San Francisco, to decide where the building should be situated.

"The secrets of positioning affect every aspect of business and personal life," the Feng Shui master reiterated as they paced the three waste-strewn lots where Charlie Wah planned to build his cafe and rooming house.

The Feng Shui master, who, in his colourful kimono and pillbox hat, truly looked like a wizard, was not telling Charlie Wah anything he didn't know. Charlie was tempted to remind him that it was he who was paying the master's train fare to and from San Francisco, as well as his substantial fee.

It was the job of the Feng Shui master, or geomancer, to detect the properties of wind and water affecting Charlie's three lots, and advise him as to the proper location of the building, the placing of doors and windows, as well as all furnishings.

To his most trusted customers, Charlie sometimes told the story of when he was a boy in China and had fallen seriously ill. His fever had run high for days as his body wasted away. With Charlie near death, a Feng Shui master was called in by Charlie's desperate family. In spite of his sickness, Charlie was impressed by the Feng Shui master's purple gown and tall cap. The Feng Shui master paced about the house allowing himself to feel the currents of life within the tiny rooms.

After a long while Charlie's mother came to his bed and whispered to him that the Feng Shui master was now at the kitchen table, hard at work with a compass and several books on astronomy.

At last the Feng Shui master announced his findings. The *chi*, or life force in Charlie's bedroom was not right. The room was hostile to male presence. Charlie was to be moved to the bedroom occupied by his twin sisters, and the bed in the sisters' room, which faced north, was to be turned to face south. The sisters, the Sheng Shui master assured Charlie's parents, would flourish in Charlie's room, for it was a female dominated area.

The instructions were followed to the letter and within hours Charlie's fever abated.

"It is vital," the Feng Shui master said, after pacing the perimeters of the property, crisscrossing several times in different directions, while staring down the hill at the bluish river that flowed sluggishly by, "that the building face perfectly north."

In order to ascertain true north, the small, bustling man worked another afternoon with his compass, jotting figures and angles in a small book he took from one of the deep pockets of his colourful gown. The problem was that in order to face true north, the Kowloon Cafe building had to sit at a very awkward angle to the street, not even close to parallel to the sidewalk, or the other buildings.

"It is also of prime importance, mandatory as it were," the Feng Shui master added, "that the back corner touch the east property line."

When all of the Feng Shui master's instructions were followed, the foundation that was laid out was of an extremely strange shape, four sided, but with all four sides of unequal length. The back corner of the east wall touched the east property line, but because of the sharp angle caused by the front facing true north, the east wall was quite short, while the rear wall of the building was actually the longest, angling across, touching the rear property line at about the centre of the three lots.

The Feng Shui master also gave advice on how the interior was to be laid out, with particular attention to the front of the building, which had, it was reported, the largest plate glass windows for a building of its size in the state. He dictated which walls the stoves were to be attached to in the kitchen, and the chimney was built in such a way that smoke would always drift to the south, regardless of the direction of the prevailing wind.

He was also specific about which direction the beds should face in the family bedrooms, differently, he pointed out, from the beds in the rooming house section, which would house transients rather than family.

"Can you believe that?" factory workers asked each other as they walked past the oddly-shaped building under construction.

"Owned by some crazy Chinaman," they said.

"Being built in the shape of a dragon," someone else said. "A pagoda," said another. "I heard it from a friend who heard the architect and the owner arguing."

After the architect reluctantly revised his blueprints and the Kowloon Cafe was built according to the specifications of the Feng Shui master, the cafe opened with a gala ceremony, the mayor cutting a red ribbon stretched across the front door. The Kowloon Cafe, complete with a red and white Coca-Cola sign covering the whole east wall, opened for business and became one of the more successful restaurants in the city.

Charlie Wah sponsored the immigration of most of his waiters and kitchen staff, young men who sat as a group eating the kitchen leftovers after their shifts had ended, then slept a few hours in one of the rooms on the second floor, before heading downstairs to work again.

The third floor was rented to single men who worked in the downtown area, and, on occasion, to transients. Many of the employed single men had the Kowloon Cafe pack a lunch for them each morning: thick meat sandwiches, a thermos of coffee, a slice of pie.

The Kowloon Cafe prospered. It catered to after-theatre and movie crowds. Charlie Wah personally called on every major business in the downtown, and as many in the suburbs as he could find time to visit, until, in the 1950s, the two banquet rooms of the Kowloon Cafe catered to almost all the Christmas parties and a high percentage of the wedding receptions in our city. Almost every wedding invitation from the mid-40s to the early-60s contained the line, *Reception dinner at the Kowloon Banquet Room.*

Over the next fifty years Charlie Wah became a very successful and respected businessman, a leader in the small

Chinese community. His eldest son worked with him in the restaurant. The three daughters and another son, born in America, excelled as students, attended Ohio State, producing a lawyer, a dentist, a stockbroker, and an electrical engineer.

As the business prospered, Charlie Wah expanded his interests to include an import-export business. He was a founder of the Chinese-American Credit Union, and, when he saw Chinese students doing poorly in school, mainly because they came from Chinese-speaking homes and were unable to master the intricacies of the English language, he contributed to, and served as an advisor to a private grade school for Chinese students, where, rather than Chinese, the students, beginning in playschool, were taught in English — the language, the customs — so that by the time they were ready to enter high school, they were more advanced in English than their American counterparts.

Still, each time Charlie Wah aligned himself with a new business or charitable venture, a Feng Shui master arrived from San Francisco to consult on the best possible location, approve the facade of the building, the placing of counters, doors and windows. The placing of the bank vault in the Chinese-American Credit Union building is a story in itself.

Most of the information I've just imparted I dug up after my first meeting with Charlie Wah. After that meeting, I called one of our corporate lawyers and asked him to use whatever means available to him to get a full personal and financial report on Charlie Wah and the Kowloon cafe.

My name is Pat Wynne. I've lived in this city all my life, and when we were awarded an expansion franchise in the National Baseball League, I became public relations director for the new club. When it was decided to acquire ten acres of riverfront property as a site for the new baseball stadium, it was one of my jobs to negotiate the purchase of several pieces of property needed to complete the site.

I first met Charlie Wah when he came to our corporate offices to discuss our purchasing his three lots and the Kowloon Cafe building. I knew who he was because I had been a customer of the Kowloon Cafe for most of my life. When I was a child, the Kowloon was still *the* place to eat in the downtown, and I first enjoyed sweet and sour ribs, tomato chicken balls, and lemon chicken in Charlie Wah's restaurant, the lacquered Chinese red and black ceiling and walls as background.

By the time I was in high school the Kowloon had been displaced by newer, fancier, more expensive Chinese restaurants, in more fashionable areas of the city. But it was still a place to take a date after a movie, have a feed of tasty Chinese food and not spend a whole week's worth of part-time income, mine deriving from the minor league baseball club I had associated myself with early. Fortunately, security was virtually nonexistent at minor league ballparks, and many of the players were local boys who held part-time jobs in the off-season — selling cars was a favourite, followed by various kinds of construction work. I just hung around and made myself useful by running errands to the concession for the players, until I sort of inherited the job of bat boy.

When I saw myself getting too old to be bat boy much longer, I made certain I knew all there was to know about equipment. The equipment manager was old and careless and I was assistant equipment manager for two seasons before he retired and I inherited his job. That was the year I graduated high school. I followed the same principles, making myself not only useful but indispensable, until I became general manager of the minor league club, and when the major league franchise was offered, I was taken on by the new owners as Vice President in charge of public relations.

I was impressed that Charlie Wah came alone to our meeting. The other merchants whose land we required all showed up with a battery of lawyers, a list of demands, and an asking price five to one hundred percent higher than what we were offering. Threats of law suits filled the air at these meetings like frightened birds.

"I am embarrassed to say," Charlie Wah said to me after we were seated comfortably, "that when I purchased the three lots for my business, I paid seventy-five dollars each for them, and probably could have had them for less because no one else wanted them. On the other hand, while I was saving to buy those lots, I was earning ten dollars a month, plus room and board.

Charlie's one concession to his origins was that he addressed me as Mr. Pat Wynne, using both my names, crushing them together until it sounded as if he was addressing me Mr. Patwin. He insisted that I call him Charlie. "Have been Charlie ever since I step on to American soil. Too late to change now."

"Anyway, the offer you've made me, which I calculate to be some fifteen thousand times my original investment, appears more than fair. As you must be well aware, the district has deteriorated over the years, until neither the land value or my business are what they once were. As a businessman I should have sold, or moved the business many years ago. But I have ties to the community . . . "

Here it comes, I thought. Instead of dragging along a lawyer in a gun-metal-gray suit, he's going to play on my heartstrings. For an extra million he'll be happy to cut his ties to the business and land.

Incidentally, the prices we were offering were about twenty-five percent below what we were prepared to eventually pay. We knew what the land was worth. Part of business is negotiation.

"I have only one request before I am willing to sign the sales contract on your terms," Charlie Wah said.

"And what is that?" I asked.

"Plans for the new baseball stadium have been drawn, have they not?"

"They have."

"You have seen them?"

"I have. A very impressive structure. I can see that you get a look at them if you'd like."

I was trying desperately to stay one jump ahead of Charlie Wah. What was he going to ask for?

"I would like that very much. I have been an avid baseball fan ever since I came to America," Charlie Wah said. "When I first came to Columbus, Ohio, I was very lonely for my wife and child, for my homeland. I eased some of my pain by watching baseball. I came across it quite by accident. I went for a walk one Sunday afternoon, my only day off work. I saw men playing this strange game on this green field. I sat down and watched for a while.

"I sat beside a man in a blue serge suit and fedora. I asked him, 'Please, could you explain what is going on?'

"The man was Jewish, his accent was as heavy as mine. We both struggled somewhat at English. But we were able to communicate.

"I became enthralled by the intricacy of the game. I was particularly impressed by the perfect dimensions of the field. Any other dimensions — if the bases were placed further apart or closer together, if the pitching mound was closer or further from the plate — the game would change dramatically, and not for the better.

"'Who invented such a wonderful game?' I asked my companion that very first afternoon. He did not know, but if I understood him correctly he said it must have been someone Jewish. I'm not positive of his reasoning on the matter, but I believe it had to do with him being proud of his heritage, therefore, he felt that something so perfectly concocted could only have been first envisioned by someone with the same history and beliefs that he held.

"Strangely, it affected me the same way, for on realizing the perfection of the layout, I knew that the field could only have been designed and approved by a Feng Shui master.

"And what is that?" I asked. "A Feng Shui master?"

"As my business became prosperous," Charlie Wah went on, waving aside my question indicating he would get to it in due time, "I took my son occasionally to see the baseball players. We would leave in the early evening, the slack after supper hours at the restaurant, and return in time for the late-evening rush. My son was as taken with baseball as I. I hoped that he might play the game. But there was little opportunity for him to do so.

"My youngest son, now that is another matter. By the time he was old enough to play baseball I was prosperous enough and knowledgeable enough to sponsor whatever team he might wish to play upon. The Kowloon Cafe sponsored Little League, Babe Ruth League, Pony League teams, still does as a matter of fact. You might have seen our uniforms, I designed them myself, what is called Chinese red numbers and piping on a white background, a fire-breathing dragon on each chest."

We were interrupted by my secretary bearing a tray with teapot and cups. I knew Charlie Wah's reputation for lengthy business discussions, most of which was not about business.

"You are too kind," he said, accepting a cup of tea. "My youngest son played four years on full scholarship at Stanford, also twice in the College World Series."

"Come on!" said Mike Peckinpaugh, when I had finished my explanation. "You're actually lobbying for us to let some Chinese guy who's part priest and part clown decide where to locate a two hundred million dollar major league baseball stadium? This Charlie Wah must have had you smoking something as well as drinking tea."

"Put it into perspective," I said. "Think about the money that can be saved if we go along with Charlie Wah. He's willing to take our initial offer for his land. The other property owners are solely interested in money. We'll bargain with them and their lawyers, and we'll end up paying about what we expected to put out in the first place.

"But Charlie is different. If he decides to block the deal he'll cause no end of trouble. If we don't play along, his price will go up by about five million, and the negotiations will drag on forever. Remember, we have to have a major league stadium finished and ready to go two years from April. We need to have everything flow smoothly. We can't change the basic location. Imagine what it will be like if we end up building the stadium with the Kowloon Cafe sitting like a monstrosity somewhere in the parking lot."

"So it is financial," said Peckinpaugh. "What's gonna happen if we don't go along? We gonna be trampled by a herd of dragons?"

"Kowloon means nine dragons," I said. "You don't necessarily see dragons," I went on, "they live in the water, in this case the river. . ."

"This guy really has you bought and paid for, hasn't he?" said Peckinpaugh.

"It isn't going to cost us anything to follow this along for a while, and it could save us a pile of cash and endless aggravation. Also, remember that Charlie Wah is a genuine baseball fan. In the long run, he wants what's best for the club."

"What's he gonna want us to do?" asked Peckinpaugh.

"Nothing we can't handle. Charlie Wah will fly in a Feng Shui master all the way from Hong Kong, rather than San Francisco. Let the Master look at the blueprints, and the drawings of the finished product. Then we'll know what kind of changes he wants us to make."

"This is crazy," said Peckinpaugh, but he reluctantly agreed to wait and see.

I walked the property where the ballpark was to be built with Charlie Wah and the Feng Shui master. The Master spoke no English. He wore a long purple gown with yellow designs on it and a matching pillbox hat. He had studied the blueprints and the drawings earlier in the day.

We traipsed along the riverbank, then around the perimeter of the entire property. The Master appeared very interested in one or two of the nearby abandoned buildings.

He spoke at length in a sibilant whisper to Charlie Wah.

"He says those buildings have bad *chi*. He says the businesses would have prospered indefinitely if there had been wider doors at the front of the building, larger windows."

"There is no way of knowing," I said.

"The Master disagrees," Charlie Wah said after another whispered conference. "He says that if these businesses had been constructed rhythmically in the first place they would still be successful, the owners would be replacing them with new and wondrous structures, and the baseball stadium would be looking elsewhere for accommodations. The Kowloon Cafe, on the other hand, is an ancient and venerable building with excellent *chi*. Unlike the other structures it has not been assaulted by dragons . . . "

"Look, I don't want to get into this business of dragons. Just ask the Master to let us know where the baseball stadium should be located?"

"A Feng Shui master will not be rushed. He will let you know his decision in good time."

Good time turned out to be three weeks, and the requests of the Feng Shui master were not untenable. The stadium, which was essentially round, was turned so the main entrance faced directly south instead of south-east. Inside the stadium the location of home plate and the dugouts were altered somewhat, but nothing the architects and owners couldn't live with. The negotiators were happy to save several hundred thousand dollars on the purchase price of the Kowloon Cafe property. Unfortunately, they did not take the Feng Shui master as seriously as they should have.

One of the Master's stipulations was that the area about the main entrance of the stadium — which consisted of rows of glass doors, beneath rows of glass windows, divided and divided again by rails of silver and gold-coloured metals, the glass in some places tinted a barely discernible blue and gold, so the windows glittered and shimmered in the early evening sunlight — was that the doors had to be much larger and higher, that the windows each be about ten times larger than shown in the plans, that the blue and gold tint be removed, the metal dividers either replaced by lacquered wood, or aluminium as close to the colour of light as possible.

I didn't know at first whether it was a deliberate violation of the agreement, or whether at some level, a gaggle of bean-counters simply saw that it would be less expensive to leave the original plans for the facade and main entrance in place. But as construction progressed, and the grid of metal material that would be filled with tinted glass emerged at the front of the stadium, it was in the original form, not the form Charlie Wah and our lawyers had worked out. As soon as the Kowloon Cafe building and property was sold Charlie closed the business and retired, though I was told he often walked along the riverbank, sporting a lacquered black cane with a gold dragon's head, apparently admiring the construction of the new stadium as it rose from its concrete foundations.

"You what?" It was my turn to be surprised and outraged. At a meeting with the architects and contractors concerning construction overruns, Mike casually mentioned that Charlie Wah had dropped by a few days earlier to question the appearance of the facade around the main entrance. From what I could gather Charlie had been dismissed in a rather cavalier fashion.

"Charlie Wah is my responsibility," I shouted. "He is a completely honourable man, and I expect him to be treated as such. He'll sue your ass. You can't brush him off."

One of the contractor's bean-counters smirked as he flipped through a stack of papers several inches thick. "We've got dual legal opinions on the matter," he said. "The facade you've proposed, Mr. Wynne, or you and Mr. Wah have proposed, is one of the sticky spots involving cost overruns. Your version of the facade, because of the stability factor needed to hold the giant sheets of glass, will be nearly three times as expensive. After closely perusing the contracts, our attorneys feel that we fulfilled our obligations by setting the stadium at the exact location Mr. Wah and yourself proposed. The business of the facade is open to interpretation, and we feel our interpretation will stand up in court."

This was the first I knew of the betrayal. I'd come directly to the meeting from the airport after being out of town for a week. After the meeting ended, while I was still protesting, I discovered there were three messages from Charlie Wah on my voice mail, his voice higher, more urgent with each call. I dialed his office, no answer, no answering machine or service. There was a page of C. Wahs in the phone book. I would have to wait until morning.

Even the weather service admitted that the storm was a complete anomaly. There were thunderclouds gathering early in the evening, thunder grumbled in the distance, a few road maps of lightning patterned the rolling black clouds. A typical thunder and lightning storm. A bitter wind whined down the river valley and, as sheets of rain inundated everything, the wind swept in off the river whipping planks through the air like toothpicks. Golf-ball-sized hail pounded the area, leaving cars with broken windshields and dented roofs. The wind and hail combined in their assault against the south face of the new stadium, twisting the grid of windows and doors into scrap in a matter of seconds.

The next morning, which was blue and sunstruck, the air crisp in the aftermath of the storm, while I was walking along the riverbank photographing the carnage with my zoom lens, who should I meet but a jaunty Charlie Wah, the dragon's head of his cane glittering in the sunshine. A team of insurance adjusters had just arrived, and were crawling in and out of the twisted building materials like children on a playground Jungle Gym.

"I honestly didn't know about this, Charlie. I've been out of town." He didn't speak, but stared at me calmly, waiting for more. "It's very important to me that you believe me. I would never go against our agreement."

"Nature, Mr. Pat Wynne, as always, appear to be the great equalizer."

"I want you to believe me. I'll put my job on the line, if it comes to that. This stadium's going to be built the way we agreed, or I won't be a part of the organization."

"I don't believe such action on your part will be necessary. The wise man learns to keep bargains or suffer the consequences."

I recalled Charlie's words. *Understanding tradition is a key to doing business.*

"I'm not certain how wise these men are." I stopped. What was Charlie Wah saying?

"You didn't have anything to do with . . . this?" I said, spreading my hands to take in the carnage that had been the front entrance of the stadium.

"Your question could be interpreted and answered in many ways. What if I were to say that there are dragons living in the river?"

"I suppose I would believe you. You have always been honest with me." I glanced at the greenish river where it flowed by with some vigour. A tugboat flowed by, travelling with the current, and its captain waved. We both responded.

"And the new facade? Why is it so important?"

"Openness is a virtue, Mr. Pat Wynne. Dragons, as you may surmise, are rather large. The open spaces are so the dragons may pass in and out as they please without causing disruption."

"I see," I replied. "Will it work?"

"Do you see any dragons?" asked Charlie.

Tulips

N ow I know how Auggie feels. Auggie is my best friend. Mutt and Jeff we were called, his second base to my right field. I'm the big one. We've played together since Little League. We finish high school soon and we had plans to head out into the world on the way to baseball careers. Though we both had a dozen or more athletic scholarships offered, only Auggie was going to college. He chose Stanford. Auggie was nicknamed The Fly for the way he buzzed around second base, sucked up anything hit to the right side, and ran the bases like they were his own personal property. A white Rickey Henderson was the way the press described him on more than one occasion. Believe me, the stands at our high school games have been top heavy with scouts the last couple of seasons. Buddy and Auggie, both headed for the Bigs. That was us.

College doesn't interest me. I had enough trouble just staying academically eligible. I can't tolerate the idea of four more years of scraping by, being tutored, ferreting out courses that don't require much skill. I'm gonna serve my apprenticeship in the minor leagues. I had seven teams seriously interested in me, but the Rockies are where I'm headed. New organization, lots of enthusiasm, huge fan support. The Rockies drafted me and we're working out a signing bonus, and where I'll start out, and what kind of coaching I'll get. I've got an agent named Justin Birdsong who is asking for more money than I dreamed possible, and he says we'll get it. Justin flew all the way to the Northwest and, just like a regular baseball scout, sat in the stands and watched us play a doubleheader against Bellingham High. He signed up both me and Auggie that same night.

"You're in the right place at the right time," Justin Birdsong assured us. "The best baseball scouts have X-ray eyes when it comes to talent, and the best have put their seal of approval on you guys. Buddy, in two years, three at the most, you'll be playing right field for the Rockies. I can't think of a ballplayer with a better future; I'm betting 40 home runs, 120 RBIs. Auggie, you'll take a year or so longer because you have a lot to learn about playing the infield and refining your natural ability as a base stealer. You're not going to hit the home runs Rickey Henderson hits, but, barring injury, you'll be breathing down the neck of his stolen base record by the time your career's winding down."

When I told Justin Birdsong about the land I intended to buy, he laughed. "Stick with me, Buddy, and you'll be able to buy this whole damn valley."

Auggie thinks that when I get my signing bonus I should buy a Ferarri, or one of those other sleek, babe-magnet cars, but I've driven my dad's old pickup too long. I've come to think of cars as a way of getting from point A to point B. I'll buy a car but probably a compact without options, something practical and as close to $10,000 as I can keep it.

I *am* going to buy land here in the valley. I'm gonna go into business with my girlfriend's father. We grow tulips. I've had the land picked out for a couple of years. I've got my wife and father-in-law picked out, too. Or, at least I did, until a week ago.

My folks want me to go for one of the scholarships.

"You need an education in this world," my dad says almost every day.

My grandfather fled Oklahoma back in the thirties. His generation's idea of heaven was a piece of land that wouldn't blow away before their eyes, and enough food so no one went to bed hungry. They found both those dreams here in this valley in Western Washington.

They sent my dad to Western Washington State University where he became a pharmacist. He was the first Claxton to attend college, ever. He married a local girl, opened up a little drugstore on main street, which he operated with some success until Wal-Mart opened up in the valley about five years ago. Now, he works for Wal-Mart and makes more money than he ever did on his own.

Auggie. Three weeks ago. A high school game. We were ahead by five. He walked on four pitches, had a big lead at first. The pitcher tossed over, nothing urgent. Auggie went back standing up. As he braced himself to stop with his foot on the bag, his right Achilles tendon snapped.

The doctors say they can fix him up so he'll probably walk without a limp. But he'll never run again. Never steal another base.

His scholarship is gone. His whole life upended.

"I could hear it snap," Auggie says. "In spite of the crowd noise, I could hear it snap just before the pain hit."

Auggie doesn't know what he's going to do. He'll probably go to WWS, though he'll have to get Work Study to make ends meet. His father drives a truck for a glass company. You know the kind: sheets of glass in slots on each side. Though he's a better student than me by far, Auggie doesn't have a clue what he"ll major in at college.

Like I said, I know how he feels. My health is still good. But I feel like I've been injured. The problem is my girl, Julie. She's broken off with me. That may seem trivial beside Auggie's problem, but I was practically a member of her family. Her dad is the nicest man I know. Everything was set. There was just no question.

If there'd been another guy, if Julie was in love with somebody else, I could accept that. But she's not.

Julie's a brain. She's going to the University of Washington, in Seattle, this fall, to study psychology. She's already read dozens of books full of pictures of the brain, and she's always talking about synapses, electrical impulses, learned behaviour, and spouting the names of guys famous for spending their lives teaching rats to ring bells. I have to admit I don't have any interest in that sort of thing, but I'd never discourage Julie from doing what she wants to do as far as college goes.

"You don't have any imagination," is what Julie said to me the night she broke up with me. Or, she might have said, "You don't have enough imagination." No. It was, "You don't have any . . . "

It was like she'd whacked me alongside the head with a brick. We'd driven up to Bellingham and had dinner at the Black Angus Steak House. I was as happy as could be. I was going to suggest we go over to Bellis Fair, the huge mall, and shop for an engagement ring, one I'd pay for when I got my signing bonus. It never occurred to me that Julie and I weren't a permanent couple. If she'd said, "Buddy, I'm in love with somebody else," it would have had the same effect, but I would have recovered.

"I've got enough imagination to picture our future," I said, trying to defend myself. "What more do I need? I think I'm a responsible guy. I'm gonna sink my baseball money into land. Your dad will farm it until my baseball career is over. I've got enough imagination to see the big old Victorian-style house we've talked about building into the sidehill down the road from your folks' place. I've got enough imagination to picture our children, all blond and rosy-cheeked like their mother. I'm not trying to hold you back. I want you to get your degree and you can practise psychology in Bellingham, or Mount Vernon, or even Everett — "

"That's not the way it works, Buddy. It's not you personally. It's the bigger picture. I shouldn't have said that about your imagination. Maybe it's more a shortness of vision . . . "

"So, I'm blind, too?"

"Oh, you're taking this all wrong."

I've known Julie since first grade. We started dating the first year of high school and, as they say, we've been inseparable ever since. Julie Vander is a farm girl, strong and healthy. Her family name was originally Van Der Linden. Her grandparents were immigrants from Holland at the end of the Second World War. Her parents were babies when they came to the United States. Their families both settled around Mount Vernon; they've known each other all *their* lives, and it hasn't hurt them a bit. Her dad's name was Johannes, which he's shortened to Joe, and her mother had a sort of unpronounceable name that was shortened to Lena.

Julie is tall, 5' 8", well built, with a rosy complexion and natural colour spots, like tulips, on her cheeks. She's a big-thighed woman who would hardly show a pregnancy. Many's the time I've run my hand up the belly of her jeans, taken hold of the waist, pulled it forward an inch or two, rubbed her belly, sometimes kissed it. "One of these days," I'd say.

"Not on your life," Julie would reply, laughing. "A long way down the road, like when I'm 25 and a psychologist. Lighten up, Buddy. We have a great sex life. Don't spoil it by rushing me."

Julie's an only child and her dad considers me the son he never had. He's told me so. He must know me and Julie have been having sex since tenth grade. All he's said to me is "Be careful of my little girl. I know I can trust you not to do anything foolish." And he'd give me a rap on the bicep. Most fathers get out the machine gun and threaten boyfriends with death if they think you've been kissing their daughters. I mean, I like Joe Vander so much that sometimes when I'm visiting Julie, I end up out in the machine shop with Joe, helping weld parts on a cultivator, or off in a shed sorting tulip bulbs.

It just never occurred to me that Julie and I wouldn't get married, just like it never occurred to Auggie that his Achilles tendon might end his baseball career before it ever started.

What if our positions were reversed? What if it had happened to me? What if I'd fractured a wrist or a shoulder, or pulled one of those abdominal muscles that take six months to heal and turn a .320 power hitter into a .200 singles hitter? And even after it's healed you're afraid it's going to go out again so you hold back, or pull off a pitch, and your average goes down as the odds of reinjuring yourself go up.

I try to imagine it.

"Concentrate on baseball," I used to tell Auggie. "Rake in

those bucks. Everything else will take care of itself."

I don't have any advice to offer him now. And Auggie doesn't offer me any advice about Julie. All we can do for each other is be friends.

It strikes me that maybe I'm more intuitive than I think I am. Or sneakier, or more self-serving.

Those are all Julie's words. The last two Julie screamed at me the night she disowned me for good. Julie wanted to leave our situation open. I'd go off to the minor leagues for Colorado Rockies, she'd study psychology at the University of Washington. We'd see each other when we could. Date others.

"If it's meant to be, we'll still be in love in five years. That's plenty soon enough to think about marriage."

"You sound like a parent," I said.

I could see Julie was going to get her way. What the hell was I going to do? Joe Vander was like a father to me. My heart grows about three sizes when I gaze across a valley ablaze with hundreds of thousands of tulips. My heart radiates heat just knowing I had something to do with them being there; the sweet, wet odours of the land are prettier and sexier than anything that can be bought at a perfume counter. Except for holding Julie in my arms or connecting with a fastball up high in the strike zone, there's no thrill like standing in a silo of tulip bulbs, their moist, mossy odour, their rough texture in my hands. I don't see the dry, dirt-caked bulb, I see the explosion of scarlet or yellow that will light the valley like sunshine come the early spring.

What really happened was, realizing I was going to lose Julie, I did something reprehensible. That's Julie's word. She used it over and over again when she found out. I made love with her twice without protection. I wanted her pregnant. I wanted her to be my wife. I wanted our child.

Half the girls in the valley are pregnant by the time they finish high school: a few accidentally, a few by mutual agreement, most sanctioned by the girl herself. When I think of some of the guys who don't want responsibility, who break and run when their girlfriends tell them they're pregnant, I'm at a loss. Why couldn't I have a girl who'd go out of her way to get pregnant because she loved me and wanted to have my child?

Why do the wrong people always seem to be together?

Julie and I have been making love for years and hasn't it been great. We call making love, *going to Miami*. That's because the Vanders took me along on a holiday one winter and Miami was hot and steamy and we had to part the air with our hands in order to walk down the street. We made love on the beach, in the ocean, behind a billboard near the motel, where we were bitten by several exotic insects, though we didn't notice until afterwards.

At home, we couldn't make love at either of our houses, and my pickup truck was anything but comfortable. Sex, however, will always find a way. We took a double sleeping bag to one of Joe's greenhouses where we spread it out beside the heater. Inside the greenhouse was like the climate in Miami, and, as we made love the clouds rolled across the valley casting mysterious shadows across us through the glass of the greenhouse. I was never so happy. We had a radio. A cooler. Even some pictures on the wall.

I can't believe I've lost her.

A couple of weeks after Julie cooled our relationship, she called me at home.

"Get over here!" she snapped.

I'd been waiting and wondering if my deception would have any consequences.

"Be right there," I said, perhaps too eagerly. I trembled with excitement. I hoped she was pregnant. I hoped she'd already told Joe and Lena. Joe would look at me dubiously, try to pretend anger, but he'd be rejoicing, too, for our partnership would be ensured, just as mine and Julie's would be. The baby would cement the two unions.

Just like staring into a crystal ball and scanning the future I'd been able to see what Julie planned to do. So, twice, actually three times, in the greenhouse we called Miami, knowing Julie would never allow me to have unprotected sex with her, I snipped the ends off condoms, donned them in the darkness under the warmth of the sleeping bag.

It seemed like the right thing to do at the time.

I was disappointed to find Julie home alone.

"I'm a week late," she said, as soon as I was inside. "What do you know about it?"

"Nothing," I protested, but try as I might I couldn't generate any shock.

Julie stared at me with a steely gaze.

"It's not a problem," I said, reaching out to touch her arm. "We'll get married. I'll always — "

"Like hell!"

"I love you," I said lamely. "It's okay."

"For you, maybe."

"For both of us. Julie, I'm gonna sign for a ton of money. You can still go to school. We can afford a live-in housekeeper so you can study, attend classes.

"Maybe I don't want a baby at eighteen. Maybe I don't want to get married . . . "

"Julie, don't be like that."

She took a step back and stared at me more harshly.

"You don't even speculate on how this could have happened, because you know how it happened, don't you?

What did you do? I know you were wearing a condom every time. You tampered with them, didn't you?"

"Those things aren't foolproof."

"*Didn't you?*" Her voice rising.

I have never been a decent liar. Eventually, I shrugged.

"I trusted you," Julie sobbed. "Even if I was pregnant with fucking triplets, I'd never marry you under any circumstances. You're reprehensible. Just get away from me," she shouted, throwing open the front door, light pouring out into the night like molten gold.

Justin Birdsong called last night. Negotiations are going well. He thinks I'll get a high, six-figure signing bonus. I've been to Denver twice and the Rockies treated me like royalty. They even flew in The Cat, Andres Galarraga, to have dinner with me, just because I said he was my favourite player. If only Julie would have come with me. I wandered around the hotel suite, turned on both TVs, sat on the sofa, lay on the bed. It should have been the happiest time of my life. *Julie. Julie.*

Auggie, who limps about with a cane, his face blank, trying not to let his confusion and disappointment show, says I should spend a chunk of my signing bonus on that famous red Ferarri we've discussed, and leave it in Julie's driveway all wrapped in silk ribbons and bows. "There ain't a gal in the world wouldn't forgive a mass murderer if he made a gesture like that."

But I know Julie, and my guess is she'd leave it to rust in the driveway until the ribbons turned to pulp, the paint began to fade and the tires rotted into the gravel.

She wouldn't take my calls or see me.

"You kids must have had some falling out," Joe said to me, after I'd walked a circuitous route to his machine shed, coming up on the property from the windowless side of the house so Julie couldn't possibly see me. "She's mad as a wet hen. I tried to put in a good word for you. But no luck."

"She'll get over it," I said dubiously.

"Hope so," said Joe, pulling his welding mask down over his face.

A week later my mother yelled upstairs to say Julie was on the phone.

"Blood won out. No thanks to you, you son of a bitch." She hung up before I could say a word.

We've closed a deal. Justin Birdsong's ten percent comes to almost a hundred thousand dollars. I called old Mr. Fetherling, the real estate agent in Mount Vernon, then Joe Vander and I went out and walked the acres adjoining his property that are for sale, but will soon be mine.

"Good land. Reasonable price," Joe Vander said, and he hung his arm across my shoulders the way a father should.

The real estate deal will close a few days before I leave. I get an invite to go to Denver to travel with the Rockies, rub shoulders with, and work out with real big leaguers for three weeks before they assign me to a minor league.

I saw Julie on the street in Mount Vernon. She was with a girlfriend. She turned her head to one side about a half block before we passed, pretending I didn't exist. I caught a whiff of her perfume. "I bought the land," I said. It was the only thing I could think of.

I've sent her letter after letter of apology. Joe says she tears them up unopened.

I was wrong. Completely wrong. Is there any way to make up for what I've done? I've thought fleetingly of sticking my hand into one of Joe's bulb planters, the cold metal cutting off a finger or two. If I showed Julie I was willing to give up all my dreams of baseball just to make up for what I tried to do to her . . . but that would be compounding one stupidity with another.

My idea is like legging it after a long fly ball, pretty sure it's going to drop for a hit, but what drives me is that the first hope is of holding the batter to a long single, and the second hope, and outside possibility, is of actually catching the ball.

As I approach Vander Farms, behind the neat white-rail fences is a long grassy knoll where Joe plants tulips that, when they bloom, spell out VANDER FARMS in magnificent red letters on a black earth background, surrounded by endless green. I got to thinking of the sign while recalling how Julie and I used to stare at it and dream that when we owned the other side of the valley, we'd spell out Julie and Buddy Claxton Tulip Ranch in huge letters that could be read all the way from the highway, and be seen all across the valley to where the mountains loom purply in the background.

At home I thought some more.

"You done the farm name yet?" I asked Joe the next day. When he shook his head I said, "Let me do it for you before I go."

"Be my guest."

But, to be certain Julie wouldn't see me working on the sign, I worked at night. Up close, the knoll is longer, steeper and taller than it looks from a distance. Each letter is more than ten feet tall, and each line a couple of feet across. There was lots of room before and after for scrollwork. It took me a lot longer than I figured. I cultivated and raked and fertilized until the hillside was smooth as black velvet.

"You could paint one of them sad-eyed children, or a snarly tiger on that surface," I told Auggie, who is still kind of stunned at his loss, like I am. Auggie walks with a cane, puzzled, hearbroken, wondering what to do with the rest of his life. I know how Auggie feels. Without Julie, I feel . . . crippled.

I laid out the letters. I needed sixteen spaces instead of the twelve for VANDER FARMS.

Julie drove by a couple of times while I was out working but never glanced my way, not expecting anyone to be working late at night on the damp, dewy hillside.

I love tulips. There is a terrible magic about planting a dirty brown bulb that looks like a dead hand, knowing that in weeks a miracle of green and scarlet, too beautiful and delicate to describe, will appear like a miracle, like a burning bush.

Like a demon under the pale moon of the valley, I arrange the bulbs. I thrust each bulb deep into the soft, moist earth. When I finish they spell out I LOVE YOU, JULIE. I'll be long gone by the time the tulips turn the knoll into a lipstick-red gash, and the message is visible for all to see. Julie won't be able to avoid looking at it every day. Maybe she'll forgive me. I don't deserve it. But then lots of people get things they don't deserve. Julie will see what I've done and maybe her heart will soften. And, far away, I'll stretch out full-length in the soft air above the outfield, as I glove a long, elusive fly ball.

The Mansions
of Federico Juarez

Federico often wakes in the night to the sickly stench of sweat and stale melon rinds. For those few seconds between wakefulness and sleep he is ten years old again, laying on a pallet on the floor of his family's tin-roofed hovel in San Barnabas, Courteguay, the syrupy air thick with the odours of poverty. Federico thinks of his hungry brothers bunched beside him in disarray, and remembers flies crawling on the closed eyes of his sleeping baby sister. He stares at his own filthy hands, his scabby feet, imagines the shoes he has never known.

Fully awake, Federico realizes that the odours are only dream and memory. He stretches, feels the security of the luxurious sheets that cover his body in the air-conditioned hotel room. The hotel room, he thinks, smiling ironically, is bigger than the hut he grew up in.

The hotel is in New York City. His team will play the Mets this afternoon. They played and beat them last night. Federico batted in his 101st run, and it is only August. He is earning four million dollars this season. He does not feel any pressure; baseball is second nature to him now. He was born with baseball skills in his blood. This is his walk year. He will become a free agent in October and his agent, Justin Birdsong, is already asking for a five year, thirty million dollar contract, and there is little doubt someone will give it to him.

Federico gets out of bed, lithe as a panther in the bluish, 4 AM light. In the bathroom he takes a bar of lavender-scented soap from his travel case, washes his hands slowly, inhaling the aroma, letting the lather cling to his fingers, allowing the clean, pure scent to carry away the last of his dream. He brings his lather-skiffed hands toward his face, feels as he does so the memories of his sweltering, hungry childhood retreat deep inside him like a stone sinking into a bottomless pool.

He goes to the phone — the hotel has 24-hour room service — and orders a club sandwich and Perrier. While he waits, he picks up the phone and dials his home in Courteguay. The telephone lines whistle and beep.

What time is it in Courteguay? Time changes confuse him. He gets the answering machine. His wife Quita's musical voice tells him to leave a message. They must be sleeping, he thinks.

"I love you, Quita," he says in Spanish. "Jorge, practise your pitching," he says to his son.

The boy is only four, but already he can stand on the miniature mound Federico has had built on the long, sloping lawn of the white-pillared mansion where they live, and hurl the ball like a midget professional. The boy loves to hear his father's voice on the machine. "Papa is inside

45

there?" he has been known to ask.

"My angel," he says to the baby, Anna Maria, "when you visit me soon, Papa will kiss each of your fingers and toes, and we will find a merry-go-round to ride."

A few months ago he'd taken his family to Disneyland. While Quita and Jorge toured the park and rides he took the baby, who was fifteen months old, for repeated rides on the merry-go-round. He stood beside her and held her in place on the bright horses with their smiling lips. His daughter laughed and cooed. Federico had never been so happy. He thinks in the second before he hangs up that he hears the baby's tinkling laughter, smells her fresh-powdered, milky smell.

He signs for his food order.

He eats at a table overlooking the neon-starred city. Taking a sheet of thick hotel stationery, Federico begins to sketch the layout of a new home, a mansion bigger than the one his family now occupies, bigger than any he has built before.

Marble, he thinks, long hallways of cool white marble.

Federico was sixteen when he was signed by his major league team. The scout was Courteguayan, a former minor league pitcher working on commission, for it had only recently been discovered that Courteguay might be a source of major league talent.

He was offered a thousand dollars to sign, a fortune in Courteguay where the annual income was about eighty dollars a year. He had been offered a thousand only because another scout had offered him five hundred a few days earlier. Federico had been thoroughly suspicious and had taken time to consider the offer.

He'd still been suspicious of the thousand dollars. He certainly would not take a check, which was what the scout had offered. Federico had never been inside a bank. In fact, no member of his family had ever been inside a bank.

He'd wanted something tangible.

"There is a house for rent, down the hill," and he pointed toward the heart of the city. Federico had walked by it many times, a small clapboard house that had, within recent memory, been painted white. The grass in the yard was bleached brown but there were guava trees in the back yard.

Federico was barefoot, his dark curls dripping sweat, his face smudged with dirt. He had just had five hits in five times at bat, one a home run, two others for extra bases. He had run the bases like a ghost, stealing three times. He'd made an over-the-shoulder catch in centre field, and later threw out a runner trying to go first-to-third on a single.

Federico sensed how good he was. He could smell greed on the scout's breath.

The house rented for 500 guilermos a month, two hundred and forty dollars a year, more than twice what his father would make in a year hauling sugar cane to the mill, if he worked steadily, which he did not.

"I want the house for my family," Federico said. He could see the scout calculating, slowly, similar to the way the palm wine vendor punched keys on his ancient cash register festooned with metal curlicues.

"Let's walk down and look at this house you desire," the scout said.

"It has two bedrooms, indoor plumbing, perhaps even the air conditioning, for sure window fans," said Federico excitedly.

How the house, far from the smoking garbage dumps, would please his mother. How many times had he heard her say, "There is poor and there is shiftless. We are only poor. Poor we cannot control. Shiftless we can."

No one in the family had ever been in trouble with the law. His older sister worked as a domestic for a family with a rich hacienda, not as a whore, like many of the girls from the slums.

After they had walked around the place, shaded their eyes and peered in the windows at the shiny tile floors, the stove and refrigerator white as twin brides, the scout, finished his calculating, said, "We will rent the house for your family for two years, AND, we will give you three hundred dollars. Your family will be able to move in by the end of the week."

"I am yours," Federico said.

Shortly, he'd found himself in America. Shoes hurt his never-before-shod feet. A small price to pay for wealth and fame, Federico thought.

Federico steamrollered through the minor leagues where the American players whined and complained about the food, which was plentiful and spectacular in variety, if bland; the hotels, which were elegant beyond his dreams, and especially the money. On his salary Federico could have lived like a king in Courteguay. Even in the minor leagues he earned more than the President of Courteguay, the mysterious Jorge Blanco.

He sent his mother eighty dollars every month. A year's worth of income to run her house. He had a telephone installed so he could call his family, tell them of his exploits, and listen to them praise him.

His one extravagance was to hire a tutor so he could learn first, to speak clear, unaccented English, then to read in both English and Spanish. He was appalled that many of the great Latino baseball players spoke only rudimentary English, and had no written knowledge of the language.

Federico remembered his childhood, the filthy sewage running down the middle of the dirt street, the taste of garbage in the air. He also remembered his father. One day when he was about seven he spotted his father hurrying up the hill a white paper bag clutched in his hand. His father had just finished work at the cane mill when a wealthy man in a limousine had asked him for directions. He'd been rewarded with a hamburger in a bag. Rather than eat it himself he had run most of the way home. He called the family together, placed the burger on a tin plate, divided it into ten wedges so everyone had a taste.

His father and mother live in their own mansion, now. They have their own cook, chauffeur, swimming pool.

If I am to be truly successful I need to be well loved, Federico thought, especially in the United States, but also in Courteguay.

From the beginning, whenever he was interviewed by the media, Federico praised his baseball organization and his fellow players extravagantly, while making light of his own accomplishments. He acquired an agent; he visited hospitals; he gave away tickets to poor youngsters.

His family was barely settled in the rented home when Federico found he could afford to buy them an even larger one. His older brother, his wife and babies remained in the rented house.

He had the scout pick out the new home, one with a stone courtyard and a high, whitewashed fence.

"You must keep one room waiting for me, Mama," he said. "A room all my own, with a high double bed, and a closet I will fill with fine clothes."

But many mansions later, Federico is still haunted by the

stifling tin-roofed hut where he was born.

$$\smallint$$

The year he was promoted to the major leagues, though his salary was still minimum, his income made him one of the richest men in Courteguay, and he decided he could afford to have a house built. Federico phoned the architect who had designed the Presidential Palace in San Barnabas. He told him how much he could afford, and thought he could hear the architect gasp.

"Something traditional," he told the architect. "I own land on a hill south of San Barnabas. White. A tall white wall to surround the tall white house. Much open space. Open air. Breeze. Air conditioning."

$$\smallint$$

Thanks to Federico there is now an eight-team professional baseball league in Courteguay, though most games are played in Miracle Stadium in San Barnabas. The original name was The Jesus, Joseph and Mary Baseball Palace of Divine Miracles, named in a time when religion still had some influence in the daily lives of Courteguayans. Each time the right- and left-wing armies exchanged power — there have been forty-seven changes in the twenty-five years Federico has lived — the stadium would be renamed

There would be a national holiday and a hundred thousand people would jam the stadium as the new right-wing dictator would re-dedicate the stadium's original name, PEOPLE'S STADIUM.

The changes in government were so frequent that people joked that the only way they could tell who was in power was to drive by the baseball stadium and see what name it bore on that particular day.

10

"No one ever mentioned to me that the government was so unstable," a *Sports Illustrated* reporter said to Federico one winter. The reporter had traveled to Courteguay to fine-tune a cover story on Federico. There had been a particularly bitter military skirmish the day before and from his hotel room in downtown San Barnabas, the reporter had seen behind the smoke from burning cane fields the sun hanging in the sky like a ripe, red plumb.

"What unstable?" said Federico. "Just business as usual. No one except the politicians themselves care who is in power. I am careful to make generous contributions to both sides. I spent nearly a million dollars to refurbish Miracle Stadium. In return both sides agreed it should become a neutral zone; the stadium is never to come under attack. Regardless of our political beliefs we all realize that the export of professional baseball players will soon become Courteguay's number one product."

"There is a joke in the United States," said the reporter, "that in Courteguay there is a factory which produces iron-armed short stops. A combination of voodoo and genetic engineering."

"I may have had something to do with starting that rumour," said Federico. "All publicity, I have learned, is good publicity."

Federico attempted to bring industry to Courteguay. He contacted a manufacturer of sporting goods and pointing to the very low labour costs in Courteguay, suggested they start an assembly plant there. The manufacturer agreed. Federico put each of his brothers in charge of a section of the plant; he found jobs for all of Quita's brothers and cousins, his own boyhood friends, and many of his mother's acquaintances, at wages higher than they ever dreamed.

His brothers and his friends complained, even though their wages were ten times the national average, that the amounts were inadequate. Two of his brothers did not think they should have to work at all. His boyhood friends complained he was cheap.

His relationship with his brothers was distant, his boyhood friends who were willing to accept charity, considered him, since he had become their employer, an enemy.

"I have done all I can. Human nature is to be ungrateful," he told Quita and his mother, who do not understand what has happened. Quita he has known all her life. She is three years younger, long legged, her skin the smooth colour of toffee. Green is her colour.

"I will buy you many green dresses," Federico promised long before he had any intimation of success. Now, he buys designer dresses, Diors, St. Laurents, and mails them to her in Courteguay.

As the first traces of pink touch the morning sky, Federico unpackages his laptop word processor. He owns a program called Floor Plan, with which he is able to draw elaborate architectural designs. He lays out a three-story, ten-thousand square foot mansion with two swimming pools, a restaurant-sized kitchen, tennis courts, a baseball diamond. He pictures the spot where this new mansion will be built. On top of a hill, about two miles from where his family now lives, but visible from that location. Federico likes to be able to stand at windows in one home and look out and see other of his mansions no matter which way he looks.

Each mansion he builds is larger than the last. Federico now owns a thousand acres of rolling green hills and valleys outside of San Barnabas. Unhappy that Courteguay is landlocked, he has built in front of one mansion a lake so large it appears to be ocean.

He admires the handiwork he has created on his word processor. As soon as the time of day is reasonable he will fax the plans to his architect.

He goes again to the bathroom, washes his hands with the lavender-scented soap. No matter how carefully and thoroughly he dries them the odours of poverty cling. He is already picturing an even larger mansion, low and flat, twenty-thousand square feet. A house so huge, so bright, so clean, that in it he will be able to escape his childhood.

Federico imagines his property stretching green and rolling to the horizon and beyond. He sees mansions, like dazzling white birds crouched on every hillside.

"Mansions are not good investments," his financial advisor, Escobar points out. "Your mansions sit empty, or are lived in by relatives. They depreciate. There are maintenance costs."

"I will never be without a clean and spacious place to live," Federico replies.

"I guess not," Escobar says haughtily. "You should run yourself through a giant copying machine, then you would be able to occupy more than one mansion at a time. Do you have any idea how many you own?"

"Yes," replies Federico. He names every one. The group in Courteguay, scattered like icebergs on the green hills, the old world mansion with fifty rooms near Newport, Rhode Island, the apartments in New York, Tokyo, Paris, the villa on the private Greek island, the ranch in Wyoming.

The road trip continues. At the plate Federico swings fluidly as if all his joints are filled with sweet oil. At bat he concentrates with a calculated ferocity, his eyes narrow but his muscles relaxed, his mind bordering on a dream state as he becomes a cat, lithe and liquid, wound tight ready to spring.

Federico remembers walking with his mother from San Barnabas toward the garbage barrio past long white walls of estates, the brilliant bougainvillea like splotches of blood, the black iron gates casting evil shadows. He would press his face against the bars to catch sight of the white sprawl of mansion beyond the manicured lawns, cool as legendary snow. Federico would think, I will. *I will.* What it was he was going to do was vague as fog and dreams, but what was clear was that he would own those gates and walls, the brick driveways, the man-made lakes, the marble mansions.

He was about eight when he discovered he could hit the ball harder and farther than boys much older and stronger. Doctors for his Major League team say his eyes, like those of Ted Williams, occur only once in ten-thousand people, their unique properties somehow allowing him a split second longer than other mortals to prepare his swing. He treats his eyes like saints, with veneration.

His team was batting in the top of the sixth inning in a game at Philadelphia's Veteran's Stadium when the call came. His worst fear was realized. Federico had often pondered what kind of tragedies he could and could not live with. What if he were hit in the eye by a fastball? He could live without playing baseball. Regardless of what Escobar said, his finances were diversified. Parents and brothers and sisters lived, aged, died. He would be heartbroken if something happened to Quita. But she had lived to rise from the garbage barrio to his mansions. He would survive. But his children were different. They were his heart and blood. Jorge and Anna Maria had not yet had the chance to live. His heart swelled every time he thought of their warmth in his arms. Could he stand to lose one of them? He didn't think so.

Before he realized it, he was on his way to the airport still wearing his baseball uniform. If he chartered a plane he could be in Courteguay before dawn. Quita had been near hysteria. Anna Maria had slipped away from her and her nanny and had fallen in one of the swimming pools. No one was certain how long she had been underwater before they found her. She was alive but unconscious, doctors working frantically. If she lived there might be brain damage.

After his arrival, he was whisked in the side door of the hospital, taken directly to Anna Maria's room. Federico was more trouble than he was useful. He blundered about the hospital offering to charter a plane and fly in specialists, to fly Anna Maria anywhere in the world for treatment.

"We are quite capable of handling your daughter's case," the doctors assured him. "Only time will tell."

He carried his grief down the hospital corridors like a fretful child.

Quita blamed herself. He tried to ease her pain, provide the comfort she needed.

Anna Maria, tiny as a doll, with ugly tubes protruding from her body lay under white sheets, still as death. While Quita dozed in a scum-green leather chair by the bed, Federico paced the room, the corridor, pushed his way through batwing doors to the waiting room.

It was crammed with family. Children scuttled about the floor, eating oranges, playing with blocks. Food odours hung like insects in the air. His sister, Corazon, was serving chile rellenos on soft tortillas. He remembered when he was very young a time when a grandmother was dying, his own mother in the waiting room of the charity hospital with a reed basket of tortillas and beans cooked on her brick fireplace. Here, Corazon had a small, white microwave oven. He could picture her burly husband, Alvarez, lugging it up in the elevator, ignoring people's suspicious stares.

His parents are there. His father holds out his hands to Federico. His silver mustache is neatly clipped as a politician's. "We are waiting," he says simply, hugging his son. His mother, dressed in black, fumbles with religious beads.

His brothers, who have hardly spoken to him — two of whom haven't even seen Anna Maria — are there, looking well-fed and grim. Federico knows their hearts flame with love for their own babies. All they can give him is their presence.

Love is all, Federico thinks, his eyes glittering. Love is all. Even in the tin-roofed hut in the garbage barrio there was love. He hugs his family. He eats, not even realizing he is doing so. He remembers the hamburger being sliced into ten pieces.

An hour later Quita stumbles sleepy-eyed into the waiting room.

"She wakes," Quita says. The family cheer.

Doctors and nurses surround the bed.

"All her vital signs are good," a young doctor says.

Federico and Quita stand beside the bed holding hands.

Her eyes open. "Papa," Anna Maria whispers, and the arm that isn't attached to the huge IV hugs his neck as he bends to kiss her.

Back in the waiting room the family begins to disperse. Federico stands at the window watching dawn tinge the horizon. He touches the cellular phone in his jacket pocket. When the time is right he will phone the architect. There are enough mansions.

Japanese Baseball

C raig Bevans knew there would be a lot of problems associated with bringing a Japanese wife to America, but as
he and his wife left Doctor Sato's office in suburban Los
Angeles, the problem the doctor had just dropped on him
was so unexpected, so much more painful than anything
he'd anticipated, that he felt stunned and disoriented as
they stepped into the noisy glare of Los Angeles in the afternoon. As they walked down the wide, low-slung concrete
steps outside the doctor's office tower, Craig's wife smiled
lovingly up at him. She took his hand, and walked so close
to him that their shoulders and thighs brushed frequently.
Craig's heart brimmed with love, while at the same moment
he felt he was going mad.

It was during his second season of Triple-A baseball in
Albuquerque — a big leaguer's batting slump away from
Dodger Stadium, the Albuquerque players joked — that
Craig's agent received an inquiry from Japan, and Craig

decided to investigate playing baseball in the Japanese leagues. In spite of Craig's impressive statistics, the Dodgers had outfield talent to burn, so it appeared his only chance of making the Big Show was a trade, something he didn't look forward to unless the trade was to a contender. But he was sure the Dodgers, being astute negotiators, would not trade him to anyone who might do them damage, and he'd end up with a non-contender, a perennial doormat, where he would waste whatever Major League career he might have left playing in obscurity.

When he met with his agent and a scout for Japanese baseball, the first word of Japanese he learned was *gaijin*, foreigner.

"Each Japanese team is allowed only two foreign players, *gaijin*, so they have to choose carefully," his agent explained. "They generally go for home run hitters. The good news for us is they're starting to look at American players coming up instead of trying to add an extra year or two to the careers of over-the-hill big leaguers."

"I don't know anything about Japanese baseball," Craig said. "I've heard it's pretty Mickey Mouse stuff."

"You heard wrong. They play good solid Triple-A baseball, pay very good money, and generally treat their players fairly. There are a few oddities, like games can end in a tie, and by American standards they mistreat their pitchers by making them throw between starts. And there's less noise from the fans, a more rah-rah, team-effort kind of attitude by the players, more college than professional.

"Japanese baseball executives have also been burned by veteran big leaguers a few times, taken advantage of by players who simply took the money and didn't put out, or they conned management into flying them home several times a year because of imagined deaths or illnesses in the family.

Japanese are very big on family, and some of these old pros spotted this weakness early on. In Japan, the baseball teams are owned by conglomerates who consider their employees family, pay for their holidays, and organize company outings. There are no trade unions of significance in Japan. The names of the teams are not the cities they come from but the corporation that owns them.

"The Dodgers feel that, regardless of how well you've done in Albuquerque, you only have warning-track power. In Japan the fences are closer in, and with warning track power here in America you could be a superstar over there. And a rich one."

The scout for the Taiyo Whales was known to the ballplayers as Knobby K. He was an American-born Japanese who had played Double A ball for a year or two in the Atlanta organization. The scout's full name was Norbu Kirinji, and he tried, too hard Craig thought, to be a good guy, to make everyone like him. Knobby K. was fast talking, hip, with Coke-bottle glasses, and a Winston perpetually lodged in the corner of his mouth.

"I've been authorized by the owners of the Taiyo Whales, specifically their general manager Mr. Sakata, to offer you a one year contract for $1,000,000, sight unseen, so to speak. It's not like I haven't video-taped you a few times. The Japanese usually like to meet their players in person before they sign them. They like the fact that you've done anti-drug commercials, and they're delighted that you're single. It's more often the wives and children who are unhappy in Japan. Many a ballplayer has been nagged out of the Japanese leagues by a family suffering from culture shock."

His agent protested that most of the *gaijin* players in Japan were much better paid.

"If you do well, the Whales will double your salary next

season. The Japanese aren't afraid to pay for performance. In fact, that will be written into the contract. You have to remember that you don't have any significant Big League experience. I don't think 0 – 7 as a pinch-hitter for the Dodgers last September is much to base salary demands on." Knobby K. beamed at his cleverness.

Craig ended up signing for $1,250,000, the amount, Knobby K. said, being exactly the absolute maximum the Taiyo Whales had authorized him to spend. Knobby K. congratulated Craig and his agent for being tough negotiators.

One of the perks negotiated in the contract, at Knobby K.'s suggestion, was what Knobby referred to as a fifteen tatami mat apartment.

"That's how apartments in Japan are measured, instead of in square footage or by the number of rooms. That's large, believe me," Knobby said. "You Westerners need space. The American concept of privacy is difficult for them to relate to, coming as they do from thousands of years of what they call 'the close proximity of generations.'"

Craig had heard stories of how unhappy many American players became in Japan. He was particularly concerned that the Americans made no effort to integrate, to learn Japanese customs or language. So, in the weeks before he went to Japan, he enrolled in a course in conversational Japanese, an act that made him realize what his predecessors had faced. Craig had never had any reason to take learning seriously. In fact, he flunked most of his final year of high school, majoring instead in baseball and girls, leaving a week before graduation to play Rookie League baseball in Medicine Hat, Canada. What Craig discovered on the first evening of the course was that either Japanese was a incredibly difficult language, or he had a mental block where foreign languages were concerned. He dropped out after three sessions.

Instead, he read the only book he could find about Japanese baseball, *The Chrysanthemum and the Bat*, as well as books on Japanese customs and history.

He left for spring training in Japan with an open mind and heart. He was determined not to be disappointed with the calibre of baseball, his teammates, his accommodation, the food. Above all, he determined to give the Taiyo Whales more than their money's worth.

As he expected, his roommate was the other *gaijin* player with the Whales, Devlin "Sleepy" Williams, a loose-boned, shambling outfielder with bible-black skin, who at 6' 7" had had his choice of careers in basketball or baseball, and had played two years as a reserve outfielder for the Yankees before deciding to move to Japan and become a star. Sleepy Williams was in his fifth year of Japanese baseball and, at 32, nearing the end of his career.

"Don't be fooled by politeness," was his first advice to Craig. "Don't mistake politeness for respect. Behind our backs business people call Americans something that translates loosely as 'meat stinkers'. *They* think *we* smell strange," and Sleepy Williams had laughed heartily.

Craig went out of his way to be sociable with his fellow players; he tried not to be pushy, and tried to fathom their customs and adhere to them. He knew he would face resentment, veiled always by courtesy, and he understood why he would be resented. He even made a valiant attempt to imitate their fish and rice diet, a move that did seem to earn him respect, though the Japanese players spoke little or no English, and communicated with Craig in primitive sign language.

"You see how it can get mighty lonely for a *gaijin* player," said Sleepy Williams. Craig agreed with him. Sleepy took Craig on a tour of nightclubs, but Craig didn't feel at home in the noisy, neon-lit clubs. Everyone seemed to drink constantly and excessively. Craig found he had his pick of young, beautiful women, who were attracted by his size, 6' 4", his whiteness, his red beard. Their excuse for approaching him was to practise their conversational English, but it soon became clear conversation was not a priority.

"They're just like Baseball Sadies back home," he complained to Sleepy. "I'd like to meet one of those girls in kimonos with the laquered-looking hair, like they show in paintings or on screens."

Suki was the first member of the Sakata family he actually met. During a practice Sleepy Williams had pointed out the Whales' general manager, Mr. Sakata. He was sitting in a box seat behind first base, a small rotund man with convex cheeks and gold rimmed glasses.

"Who's the bat girl?" Craig had asked Sleepy. "The Japanese seem so straitlaced I'm surprised they allow a girl on the field.

"That's Suki, the general manager's daughter. Apparently, if you're rich you can do anything you damn well please."

"How does a Yankee like workin' for the Japanese dollar?" Suki said to him while he was choosing a weapon from the bat rack.

"The pay is good," Craig said. "But I'm happy to meet someone who speaks English. I'm not very adept at learning Japanese."

"I can teach you," said Suki. She was a bouncy girl of perhaps eighteen, in shorts and a Whales uniform jacket, her hair in a ponytail. "I'll teach you a greeting for when my father invites you to dinner. He always invites the *gaijin* players to our house. When he introduces himself I'll teach you to say 'Get lost, Fatso,' in Japanese."

"I might find myself back in the States if I said that."

"Right. How about if I just teach you to curse in Japanese?"

The batter popped out to first base. Craig moved toward the on-deck circle.

"I'll teach you tell jokes: How many *gaijin* does it take to change a light bulb? And watch out for Japanese girls, they're all looking for rich American husbands."

The season opened and Craig batted .400 in his first month as a Whale. He was interviewed constantly, but was unable to read the stories that appeared below his picture in the newspapers. He bought a car, and did a lot of exploring, most of it alone, though Sleepy Williams occasionally accompanied him. The team went on its first long road trip, and Craig's success continued. Two months into the season, as Suki had predicted, he received an invitation to dinner.

"Bow a lot and smile a lot," was Sleepy's advice. "Take little presents for the Sakatas. And be careful how you word what you say. Suppose you admire a painting or a vase: your host is liable to say 'It is yours, my friend.' That's just a way of making polite conversation. You haven't actually been given the piece of art work. So don't embarrass yourself by trying to take it home with you. It's happened, and caused a lot of uncomfortableness to all concerned. If they offer to give you something, say, 'You are too kind,' and leave it at that."

Craig arrived at the Sakata home exactly on time. The house was very impressive, located in an exclusive suburb. A maid ushered him into a room where he was met by Mr. Sakata, who after a few moments of polite conversation introduced Craig to his wife, who was dressed conservatively in Western clothing, and disappeared after a few pleasantries had been exchanged. A bit later Suki bounded into the room wearing a tennis dress and a headband. He felt more comfortable in her presence; he was used to her being around the ballpark. As well as acting as bat girl during practice games, she sometimes hit ground balls to the infielders. Suki was usually dressed in jeans and a T-shirt, the arms of a sweater knotted around her waist. She breezed in and out of the clubhouse, her ponytail bobbing, her glasses on the end of her nose, unaware or indifferent to the embarrassment she caused the players she stumbled on in various stages of undress.

After dinner Suki grabbed his hand.

"Let me show you the rest of the house," she said. "There's someone else I want you to meet. I'll bet the folks haven't even mentioned Miyoshi to you."

There followed a sharp exchange in Japanese between Suki and both parents.

"What was that all about?" Craig asked when they were safely in another part of the house.

"Nothing to worry about. They like to think they're pretty modern parents, but they aren't really. They weren't going to have you meet Miyoshi, at least not on your first visit."

"Who is Miyoshi?"

"My sister. She's three years older than me; she's been raised as a traditional Japanese girl. She doesn't speak

English. She hasn't been to university. 'Little Flower', Daddy calls her. Miyoshi arranges flowers, which is an art form here in Japan in case you hadn't noticed. Miyoshi dresses beautifully and looks like she stepped right out of a dream."

Craig couldn't tell from Suki's tone if she was simply relating facts or if she was speaking with irony.

"I take it you don't arrange flowers," he said.

"Boring, Craig-san. I'm going to work in the stock market, after I go to graduate school in the US."

The room where they found Miyoshi was stark: pillows, mats, a low-slung table, a screen with long-legged herons pointing their beaks at a tranquil sky. There was a middle-aged woman in the room, also dressed traditionally. She vanished after a nod and a word from Suki.

"Mrs. Oma, Miyoshi's maid," said Suki.

Miyoshi bowed and averted her eyes when Craig was introduced.

For an instant Craig was glad of the language barrier, for surely he would never think of anything to say to Miyoshi, he was that attracted to her. Her hair was dressed in the traditional manner. She wore a kimono of the palest blue silk, which Craig recognized from the books he had looked at as being in the thousand cranes pattern. Her hands were tiny, her features even and unblemished. When she spoke with Suki her voice was soft and modulated, her smile so sweet Craig decided on the spot he wanted her smile to be for his eyes only.

"Would it be alright to tell her that I think she is very beautiful?" Craig asked Suki.

Suki spoke to Miyoshi, who smiled and bowed again, blushing noticeably as she did so.

"Don't get any ideas there, *gaijin* ballplayer," Suki said, poking Craig's arm. "Miyoshi doesn't get out in the real world. She leads a very gentle life. You wouldn't know what to do with a girl like her."

"Treasure her," said Craig. He could feel his pulse throbbing in his throat. He tried to say a few words in Japanese, but Miyoshi smiled shaking her head, not comprehending. She looked to Suki to translate. Suki said a couple of phrases, and Miyoshi laughed aloud, again averting her eyes.

"What did you tell her?"

"I said you've fallen in love with her and you want to take her away to a land where everyone is a red-bearded giant like yourself."

"And what did she say?"

"Miyoshi thinks you look like a prince from a fairy tale."

"Maybe I am. I feel like a prince when I look at her." Craig closed the distance between them. He held out his hands to Miyoshi, who stood and let him take her hands. She was so tiny. Craig could feel the blood rush to his hands as they touched. They bowed to each other. Craig brought one of her hands to his lips and kissed it. "Would it be a terrible breach of etiquette for me to ask Miyoshi for a date?"

"You'd have to talk to Daddy about that," said Suki, smiling mysteriously.

Craig met Sleepy for lunch the next day.

"Do you know Suki has a sister?" were his opening words.

"No. But hum a few bars and I'll fake it."

"Seriously."

"I had no idea, man. I always thought Suki was an only child."

"She has a *Japanese* sister."

"Last time I looked Suki was Japanese."

"She has an old-fashioned Japanese sister. Miyoshi looks

as if she stepped right out of a Japanese screen. It's like there is a beautiful peachy haze surrounding her. On hazy days back home on the Oregon coast my mother would look out over the ocean and say, 'Oh, it's so Japaneezy out there today.' Miyoshi doesn't speak English. Seldom goes out. She has a maid who dresses her hair in traditional Japanese style, and she dresses traditionally, too. Last night she was wearing a kimono in the thousand crane pattern; I recognized it from one of the books — "

"Sounds to me like you're more than casually interested in this sister."

"Miyoshi! Doesn't her name have a sweet sound to it? I guess I am interested in her. Must be a surprise for the Sakatas. I'd guessed I was invited to their home because Suki was interested in me."

"Don't be too sure," said Sleepy. "The Japanese never take chances. They plan every detail; they research. Nothing is ever left to luck."

"But love is an intangible. It can't be counted on."

"Don't be too sure," said Sleepy.

Two days later, as full of apprehension as he had ever been, Craig knocked at the door of Mr. Sakata's office at the stadium. After exchanging pleasantries Craig said, "I have something important I would like to discuss with you." Craig always found himself speaking in stilted and formal English when he communicated with the Japanese, as if speaking that way would make him easier to understand.

"And that is?"

Mr. Sakata looked very small behind his large chrome and glass desk.

"First of all I want to say how much I enjoy playing baseball for the Whales, and how much I appreciate you and your family going out of your way to make me feel welcome."

"You are too kind," said Mr. Sakata.

"I want you to know how much I admire the management and owners. I realize that business and pleasure, especially involving an outsider, a *gaijin* such as myself, do not ordinarily mix." Craig wondered how long he could keep talking in such an unfamiliar way. "However, in view of your hospitality and your interest in my personal well-being, unworthy as I am, I wish to ask your permission for me to call on your daughter and ask her out. Ask her for a date," Craig added when Mr. Sakata gave no sign of having heard him.

Mr. Sakata sat silent for a long time, his small hands loosely joined as they rested on his shining, empty desk. Finally he spoke, choosing his words as carefully as Craig had chosen his.

"It is true that while we strive to make visitors feel welcome, we also maintain a respectable distance from outsiders. However, I am not certain that what you ask lies within my powers anymore. You have met my daughter both at home and at the stadium. You are aware that she is a modern girl, one who makes her own decisions, lives her own life. While Suki tolerates tradition, she would not take kindly to my arranging a date for her. You will have to ask her yourself."

"I apologize for not making my intentions clear. I agree that Suki is a modern young woman with a mind of her own. But it is not Suki I wish to date, it is Miyoshi."

"Ah," said Mr. Sakata. If he was taken by surprise he did not show it. "Miyoshi is an old-fashioned Japanese girl. Miyoshi does not speak English." He stopped and stared at Craig, expressionlessly, as if his statements were explanation enough.

"I am trying to learn Japanese, though I admit my progress is not good." He stared back at Mr. Sakata.

"Miyoshi?" Mr. Sakata remained silent for the longest time, his eyes closed. Craig could hear his own breathing. Finally Mr. Sakata spoke again. "Yes, I believe it would do Miyoshi good to see more of the real world."

Craig recognized implied consent when he heard it. I can play the game too, he thought.

"Unworthy as I am, I will try to make the experience pleasant for Miyoshi."

"Ah," said Mr. Sakata.

Craig at first used Suki as a translator. She explained to Miyoshi that Craig wanted to take her out, and after Miyoshi didn't refuse the invitation, Suki accompanied them on their first two dates, one to dinner at an expensive restaurant, and the other to a movie, which, when he actually paid some attention to it, Craig intuited was a comedy about an inept detective.

Next, through Suki, he invited Miyoshi to a baseball game. Mr. Sakata looked sharply at both he and Suki when she explained what was happening, but then his face returned to its usual calm. Miyoshi sat in the special seats Craig had reserved behind the Whales dugout. He thrilled as she pointed at him in delight when he emerged from the dugout. He watched as Suki explained the goings-on to her. He watched Suki pull Miyoshi to her feet as Craig lashed a hanging curve ball into the right field seats.

On their outings Craig would catch Suki watching him out of the corners of her eyes. He wondered what she was keeping from him. He even entertained the idea that Suki was in love with him until he remembered that it was Suki who went against her parents wishes to introduce him to Miyoshi.

A few weeks later, for three consecutive days Sleepy Williams accompanied Craig and Miyoshi to a Sumo Tournament.

"The only sport that's more pure than baseball," Sleepy said, on the drive to the arena.

Craig laughed at the idea, but after an hour of witnessing the splendorous bravado 'of the pre-match rituals and ceremonies, then the contests, the two huge men in a measured circle, the winner the man who forced any part of his opponent out of the circle or forced any part of his opponent other than the soles of his feet to touch the earth. Miyoshi loved the sumo matches; though the spectators, much like at a baseball game, were subdued, polite beyond imagination. Craig and Sleepy cheered for their favourites, as did Miyoshi, clapping with childlike enthusiasm when a wrestler she liked won his match.

"The appeal of Sumo is that there are no bad guys. Everyone is totally honourable," said Sleepy. "Fans have favourites, but you cheer for your favourites, never against their opponents." Craig quickly understood the concept, and it appealed to him.

When love was involved, language was not the barrier Craig had imagined. From the first time he'd tentatively held Miyoshi's hand, it became apparent that the language of touch was all they needed. There was never any doubt that Miyoshi returned his affection, even loved him. She conveyed her love by touch, by gesture, by the way her thigh brushed against his as they walked, by her smile, by the way she eagerly fitted herself into his arms.

Laboriously, Craig learned to say 'I love you', in Japanese, practising with Suki, who seemed genuinely delighted that her reclusive sister had found someone to love. When he spoke the words to Miyoshi, she spoke several sentences he did not understand, though the tone was unmistakably positive. To make certain she was not misunderstood Miyoshi made herself available to be kissed.

When he held her, Miyoshi felt light as a butterfly in his arms. Craig would kiss her neck while she giggled prettily, his trimmed beard tickling her. Then they would kiss. Finding wonder in physical contact, Miyoshi acted as if each experience was new to her, which, Craig decided, it probably was.

"There is a proverb," Sleepy Williams said, "something about every Japanese girl being ten thousand times a virgin."

Suki took care of breaking the news to her parents that Craig and Miyoshi wished to marry at the end of the baseball season. The news was received with detached solemnity. Mr. Sakata offered to coach Craig concerning the groom's role in the traditional Japanese wedding service. Craig surmised that since the Sakatas were rich there would be a large wedding, but Suki explained that her parents felt it would be immodest to stage such an event. There would be only the Sakata's immediate family, and, if he felt it necessary, his own parents and siblings. Though it wasn't true, Craig told the Sakatas that his family would feel uncomfortable in Japan, that they weren't prepared to make the long trip. He told the Sakatas he would take Miyoshi to America to meet his family immediately after the honeymoon. He wondered if the Sakata's reticence to celebrate the marriage had to do with his being a foreigner.

71

"Don't be paranoid," Suki said. "The family is delighted to have a rich baseball player for a son-in-law."

🟡

The baseball season was a triumph for Craig. Though the Whales played barely .500 baseball, he averaged .341, hit 37 home runs, drove in 101 runs, stole 46 bases. He was named most valuable *gaijin* player in the league.

🟡

"Miyoshi is used to being taken care of," Mr. Sakata said to Craig a few weeks before the wedding. "I hope you understand. Her personal maid will of course travel with her at all times, and will live with you after the marriage."

"On the honeymoon?" Craig asked.

"Miyoshi is not used to taking care of herself," Mr. Sakata reiterated by way of explanation.

Craig, trying to act with less surprise than he felt, quickly agreed. I'm glad I'm earning big money, he thought, considering the extra room, the wages. And the woman herself, an expressionless, silent person of indeterminate age, who spoke no English, and seemed to regard Craig with the defeated tolerance one extends to a large, unwieldy pet.

"I'll have to arrange for travelling papers," Craig said, but Mr. Sakata waved the thought aside.

"Already taken care of," he said. "You and Miyoshi shouldn't have to trouble yourselves with details. As is the honeymoon," added Mr. Sakata, producing airline tickets and hotel reservations for three weeks in Hawaii.

"It is really nothing," Mr. Sakata said, a half smile creasing his face. The airline is an admirer of good baseball and were only too happy to provide tickets for a star player such as yourself, and the hotel, well, let me say I am what you would call a major shareholder."

"I believe it will be good for Miyoshi to live in America," said Mr. Sakata, a few days before the wedding.

"I'm certainly going to take her home for a visit. We'll fly from Hawaii to Oregon to meet my family right after the honeymoon."

"I'm afraid I meant more than that," said Mr. Sakata. "You will receive a communication from your agent very shortly. It is fair to inform you that the Whales and the Los Angeles Dodgers have engaged in much discussion lately. The Dodgers, because of a serious and career-ending injury to one of their stars, now have an opening in their outfield, and they have begged us to allow them to buy you from us, or failing that to allow them to negotiate directly with you. It is only fair to tell you that a deal will be consummated shortly."

"But I thought you were happy with my play, and the Dodgers don't feel I have enough power for the National League," said Craig.

"Happy? Of course we were happy with your play. You are a great baseball player and an honourable man. We admire you so much we would not stand in your way of playing in America at, I may add, three times what we are able to afford to pay you. I should also tell you there has been a Dodger representative following the Whales, measuring the distance of every home run you hit this season. They have changed their evaluation of you."

"It seems that none of these events come as a surprise to you. You're not unhappy that I'm going back to America? You understand that Miyoshi will go with me?"

"Bitter and sweet must always mix. It is sad because you are now part of my family, and because you will take my beautiful Little Flower across the ocean. But the sweet of it is that your financial position will improve vastly, and you will be given the chance to be a hero in your own land."

There was something too pat about the whole situation.

Craig recalled Sleepy Williams' words: "The Japanese never take chances, they plan every detail, they research, they rehearse."

10

In America, even more than in Japan, the formidable old woman guarded Miyoshi like a treasure. Mrs. Oma spent more time with Miyoshi than Craig did. They chattered like schoolgirls, worked at sewing and flower arranging; the old woman cooked Japanese food for Miyoshi, and the kerosene-like odour of the hibachi filled the house. The old woman seemed to hold Craig in mild contempt, and treated him like a benign intruder. Craig thought he could feel her jealousy in the air when he took Miyoshi's hand and led her off to their bedroom. The old woman dressed Miyoshi's hair every morning, a task Craig noted Miyoshi did not seem capable of doing herself. There were so many things Miyoshi did not understand. Craig had acquired a vocabulary of perhaps fifty Japanese words, while Miyoshi on the other hand seemed to have acquired no English other than his name.

If he came into a room where they were, the old woman ignored him, while Miyoshi smiled, and rising, came forward to be kissed. Miyoshi would pour him a bowl of Japanese tea, offer him almond cookies. If the old woman intuited that Craig intended to stay she would rise, and bowing silently, first to Miyoshi then to Craig, take her leave. She must, Craig thought, realize by the way I look at Miyoshi that

I truly love her. One afternoon when he and the old woman were left alone, Craig studied her carefully, trying to understand her. The woman, who was not as old as he imagined — only fifty-eight according to her passport — had no life of her own. It was as though she existed solely to tend to Miyoshi.

Craig poured himself a bowl of tea, then noticing that the woman didn't have any, he poured a second bowl, and taking it in both hands, bowed to the old woman and placed the bowl in front of her. Though she tried to remain expressionless there was the hint of a smile in her old eyes as she accepted the tea and raised the bowl to her mouth.

Miyoshi was a compliant if not ardent lover. During their courtship she loved to kiss and cuddle, often becoming quite passionate in the few moments they managed to be completely alone. Initially, Miyoshi seemed genuinely surprised at the sex act and all it involved. Surely Suki or the old woman, or even her mother had prepared her for what marriage entailed?

In Los Angeles Craig rented a two-bedroom house in Benedict Canyon, promising Miyoshi they would soon shop for a home of their own, or if that failed have a house built.

His second week back in America Craig found himself on the phone to Japan.

"Suki, I don't think Miyoshi is happy here. I'm learning a few more words of Japanese, but she seems uninterested in learning English."

"Maybe Miyoshi doesn't need to learn English?"

"I want to be able to have a conversation with her."

"It would be easier for you to learn Japanese. Miyoshi is very delicate."

"Not that delicate. As soon as we moved into the house I enrolled her and Mrs. Oma, in an ESL course. They only went once. After that Miyoshi made it clear, through Mrs. Oma, that she didn't want to go again."

"Some are not able to master foreign languages," said Suki. Her way of saying "Ah."

"Look I want to have a conversation with my wife. I've hired someone to tutor me in Japanese. I start in two weeks. In the meantime I called the American Medical Association, and they've put me in touch with a psychologist who speaks fluent Japanese. I want to know what Miyoshi's thinking."

"It would be better if you didn't do that," said Suki.

"Why not?"

"Some people are not able to master foreign languages," Suki repeated, effectively ending the conversation.

"I realize the problem is mainly mine," Craig told the psychologist, a Dr. Sato. "I'm going to learn Japanese if it kills me. I start a crash course next week. Miyoshi, unlike most young people in Japan is not dying to try out her conversational English."

"Let me talk with her alone," Dr. Sato said.

"I don't know how to phrase this delicately, Mr. Bevans," Dr. Sato said as he emerged from his office an hour later. "But . . . are you aware of Miyoshi's . . . problem?"

"Only that she has as much trouble learning English as I have learning Japanese."

"I'm afraid it's much more serious than that."

"What do you mean?"

"You are not aware that Miyoshi has suffered an injury?"

"What injury?"

"This is very difficult for me to say, but when Miyoshi was about seven years old she was struck by an automobile. She suffered serious head injuries. As near as I can determine her mental growth stopped at that point in time."

"You mean she's retarded."

"She has suffered severe brain damage."

"But why wouldn't someone tell me? Her parents are rich. She wasn't a burden on them."

"There are so many subtleties, Mr. Bevans. In traditional Japanese families it is of paramount importance not to lose face."

"The Sakatas were ashamed of having a brain-damaged daughter?"

"There are so many subtleties . . . incidentally, though I'm sure it is very early, without conducting any tests I'm virtually positive that Miyoshi is pregnant."

"Well, I'll take her back to Japan. She should be near her family. I wonder how much she understands of what's happened to her? I love her; I can learn to adjust. I intend to stay with her."

"I'm afraid your inclination to take Miyoshi back to Japan won't be possible."

"Why?" Craig was standing, staring down into Dr. Sato's delicately-boned face.

"The Sakatas, though I'm sure they were very kind to Miyoshi, felt inferior because of what had happened to her. In other words they lost face. You, on the other hand, though you had no idea of the situation, lost face by marrying her. No, you cannot return to Japan. You would not find a position open to you in Japanese baseball, though I'm sure after your career is over, if you need a job one will be found for you in America, with a Japanese corporation."

9

On the drive home Craig found his eyes filling with tears each time he looked across at Miyoshi. As he pulled into his driveway, Miyoshi slid across the seat. She wiped a tear off his cheek with a tiny finger, and held her face up to be kissed. Craig held her close for a long time before they went into the house, where he wasted no time getting Mr. Sakata on the phone.

"Do you wish to return her?" Mr. Sakata said to Craig after listening to his recital of grievances.

"No. Of course not," snapped Craig. "She's not a VCR. I just wish you'd been honest with me."

"You would have considered Miyoshi as one eligible to become your wife if you had known all the details prior to your first meeting?"

"There's no way to know that, is there?"

"Ah," said Mr. Sakata.

The transcontinental static roared above the conversation. It was as if the telephone receiver was a sea shell pressed against Craig's ear. Emptiness reverberated like an enormous gulf.

The Indestructible
Hadrian Wilks

I ache.

"Again, Liebowitz? You are the clumsiest man on the face
of the earth, already," Dr. Harvey Sarner says to me.

I am at the hospital. It is 2 AM

"I need stitches. I would rather you sew me up than the
intern here who looks twelve but must be all of sixteen. They
don't let them operate on people until they turn sixteen do
they?"

I had at first a small qualm at calling my friend Sarner at
2:00 AM Then I considered that over the years my injuries
have paid for his condo in Key West. For me he should be
delighted to get up at 2:00 AM to suture above, and maybe
below, my right eye. Also, Sarner is the only one I've talked
to seriously about my being possibly possessed by a dybbuk.
To my wife, Bernice, I have mentioned this possibility, which

she dismisses as nonsense. Bernice is not much on either Hebrew mythology, or religion. She worships her Saks Fifth Avenue credit card, her charge at Tiffany's.

"Oy, Liebowitz, you should be clumsy in the middle of the day instead of always the dark of night?"

"I am occupied by a dybbuk. A dybbuk, a wandering soul, works at night. However, three hours I've been holding a handkerchief to my face at Emergency. Only now are my X-rays back. I have a cracked cheekbone, a chipped tooth, a swollen lip, gravel embedded in my hands and knees, and cuts above and below my right eye."

"You fell down again, yes? I have ninety-year-olds who fall down less. You are in the prime of lifFe, Liebowitz. Try to stay on your feet."

I am only thirty-eight, the same age as Hadrian Wilks, the famous baseball player. Geminis both of us. Wilks eight days younger than me. My waist is thickening, there is a tinge of gray at the temples of my longish blue-black hair. Bernice, who is dark and tall, who looks stunning in green, says, "Yossi, you are handsome, sexy, virile." I am flattered. She has her sights set on a chestnut Mercedes the colour of her eyes. She will get it.

"I fell down coming out of the ballpark. Tripped on a parking barrier, stumbled for twenty feet before I crash-landed on my face. My glasses are broken in half, the lenses gouged."

"And Hadrian Wilks?" asks Dr. Sarner

"Tonight I thought I had been spared. I'm listening on my radio to the Yankee game in Kansas City. Two hours earlier there. I sit in Shea Stadium watching them lose to Atlanta. On the radio, in the seventh inning, Hadrian Wilks gets hit in the face. 'Oy,' says the announcer, 'blood everywhere.' They drive an ambulance right onto the field to gobble up

Hadrian Wilks and transport him to the hospital. At Shea Stadium, I'm sitting unharmed in my seat. I look above me, scan the dark sky in case something should fall on me. One of them damn planes, maybe, in and out of La Guardia all night like mechanized buzzards, every game.

"'Looks like for sure Hadrian Wilks' consecutive-game streak is over with only fifty-one games until he passes Cal Ripkin's record,' says the announcer. The Mets game ends. I walk more carefully than you can imagine. Rude people everywhere, young thugs running, rough-housing. In Kansas City the game goes on; they await a bulletin on Wilks' condition.

"I make it to the parking lot. I dodge cars. I dodge people. I am careful like you wouldn't believe. I see my car. I make a beeline for it. Suddenly, in front of me a parking barrier that wasn't there five seconds ago. I trip, I stumble, I fall. Next thing, two guys are leaning over me.

"'You alright, Mac?' one of them says.

"'Do I look alright?' I ask, groping for my glasses, blood dripping in my eyes. They help sit me up, then wander away, eyes downcast when I ask for further help. Everyone else ignores me. I look like a drunk who has fallen. Eventually, I make my way back to the stadium, to emergency medical, where a nurse wipes the dirt and blood off my face. 'You got some nasty bruises, scrapes.' She puts antiseptic on my hands, on my knees, right through the shredded cloth of my slacks, brand new, second time I wore them. 'You're gonna need stitches,' she says. She gives me directions to the hospital. Do they offer they should pay for a cab? Give to me a subway token? Neither."

"Sit tight. Twenty minutes, I'll be there," says Dr. Sarner. "And Wilks? You heard yet his condition?"

"The game just ended. Wouldn't you know, not so serious

as first thought. A badly bruised cheekbone. Nothing broken. He'll at least be able to pinch hit tomorrow night. His
streak's alive!"

"And him not even Jewish."

"A Righteous Gentile, perhaps."

"So what's he done good for Jews, Yossi?"

"Is married a Jewish girl. You should know that, Sarner."

"Is good for Jews he should marry a Jewish girl?"

"He refused to play golf at a country club wouldn't admit
Jews. He gives to good causes. To Israel some. I've seen the
canceled checks. Sometimes is an advantage to be a partner
in a multinational accounting firm."

I was ten the first time it happened to me. Hadrian Wilks I
knew from nothing. I was playing Little League. For a pudgy
kid with glasses I was average. I could hit the ball. I ran with
the speed of water finding its own level. In the second
inning, as I batted, I took one right in the middle of the
forehead. Next thing I am boots up in the dust, the umpire
staring into my face. The stickiness when I touched my forehead I knew was blood. More stars than the planetarium. A
night in hospital for observation. Five stitches. I am dizzy for
days. My mother keeps me from baseball for two weeks.

It is only three years ago, after I become suspicious, that I
read in a story about Hadrian Wilks that when he was ten he
was hit in the forehead by a pitch, rushed to hospital.
Doctors, even then, marvelled that he needed only one
stitch, a night for observation he spends, no dizziness, his
eyes are fine. He plays ball the next day.

I have had more injuries than any accountant should suffer: every kind of sprain and muscle pull known to medicine. In high school I broke both ankles: one at a time,

thankfully. Once, playing softball, when I slid into a home plate made of concrete, the other slipping on water as I took the two steps down from the cafeteria.

"Liebowitz, you are the clumsiest student on earth. Our medical insurance premiums rise simply because you are with us. They know about you," says Feldman, the principal.

と

On my honeymoon a rock falls from a cliff in Arizona and paralyzes my elbow. A bone spur. Surgery I need. "You'd think you were an athlete," Dr. Sarner said to me after the operation. "Such bone spurs come usually after pitching 200 innings a season."

That was my introduction to Harvey Sarner.

と

Who is Hadrian Wilks? Fifteen years ago he came to the major leagues. I'd heard his name a few times, touted by those in the know as a coming superstar. His streak started in his second season. He'll break Cal Ripkin's record for consecutive games in late September. He has been under a media spotlight for the last three years as he passes Lou Gehrig, closes in on Ripkin. It came on me like a biblical revelation, about two years ago, that my pattern of injuries coincided with those of Hadrian Wilks. The Indestructible Hadrian Wilks as he has come to be called. He gives the sportswriters a thrill a game. Wilks plays with total abandon, as if the approaching record never enters his mind. He doesn't like to come out of a game, though as long as he appears on the field in a game, he inches toward the record.

"I don't want the record tainted," he says. "I want to play every inning possible."

He plays like there is no tomorrow. He leaps into the stands behind first base after foul balls, topples into the dugout if a play calls for it. Still, at 38, he steals an occasional base, sliding into second like a charging bull. No one knows better how to take out a second baseman in order to break up a double play. He has had so many injuries. He plays through them. The sportswriters love him, the fans love him. He is one of the most popular players ever to put on a uniform.

10

We are walking across the parking lot, me and Sarner, late as always; Harvey considers half an hour late, early. Doctors are used to keeping people waiting. Sarner is soft as a baby, lists forward, pulled that way by the extra weight he carries on his belly like a pregnancy.

"A fine example for your patients," I have chided him.

"A love affair with pie and ice cream," he says, shrugging amiably. "Lori prefers I should be enamoured of food rather than other women."

Sarner may well have married one of the world's most beautiful women. Doctors get all the breaks that way. While Sarner puffs up like he's snake-bitten, Lori not only fails to age, but becomes more beautiful as the years pass.

We are listening to the national anthem on Harvey's transistor radio. By the time we buy tickets and find our seats, we will have missed Hadrian Wilks' first at-bat.

"Muddy Corcoran takes his final warm-up pitch and Hadrian Wilks steps into the batter's box," the announcer says while we shuffle toward the ticket window.

"Corcoran looks awfully sharp tonight," the announcer goes on. It's not that he has such wonderful stuff, but the way he delivers. He hasn't been called the "Octopus" all

84

these years for nothing. Corcoran is all arms, legs, knees and elbows, making it almost impossible for the batter to pick up the ball as it leaves his hand. Corcoran has always had a tremendous advantage over the hitters: consider his 2.80 ERA over his seven year career.

"Here's the first pitch, it's in on . . . Oh, it hit him. It hit Wilks in the face. He's down writhing in the dirt. The trainer and manager are at his side. Oh, it looks like he took it on the right cheek. There's blood everywhere. Wilks is still now. It appears he's lost consciousness."

We are still fifty yards from the front of the stadium.

"Damn," says Harvey Sarner, and steps up his pace.

"Slow down. I'm the one in danger here.

"They're bringing a stretcher out on the field. This looks bad. His teammates are gently lifting him onto the stretcher. Manager Schmidt is holding a towel against Hadrian's face. The towel is already soaked through with blood. It looks like this signals the end of Hadrian Wilks' incredible string of consecutive games."

The announcer describes how Wilks is closing in on Cal Ripkin's record, and how before that Lou Gehrig held the record for fifty-some years, and once he passes Ripkin there will be only fifteen games to go to pass the all time record holder, Winslow Martinez, the white-eyed shortstop from Courteguay, who was rumored to be bionic, or perhaps voodoo-induced. Martinez never in his career allowed himself to be examined by anyone in the medical profession. "It is my diet, mon, he told reporters thousands of times over the years. "High in guava, low in fat, my bones bend like a baby's, never break, my skin is thicker than a leather belt."

Proceeding quickly but cautiously, I keep my eyes on the entrance to the stadium, when from behind I'm taken out by a hoodlum on a Jetpower Board, the latest machination of evil manufactured specifically for teenagers. The rider bears so much armor he looks like something directly from the futuristic movie *Rollerball* — a movie, incidentally, whose time has come.

"Are you alright," Sarner asks stupidly, as he kneels beside me.

"I should know how I am?" The world spins dizzily. "Aren't you the doctor? You figure out how I am."

I lie with my right hand under the right side of my face. Blood is oozing through my fingers, dripping on the grit-covered asphalt, a small pool forming.

"Today, for Hadrian Wilks was consecutive game number . . . " I miss the exact total as a horn honks behind us. "He's been called Indestructible for so long it's like a second name. The ambulance is pulling in from left field. Corcoran is walking alongside the stretcher. Off the field he and Hadrian Wilks are best friends. There was no ill intent. Just a curve ball that got away. In fact, I believe Hadrian was best man at Corcoran's wedding a few years ago.

I lie perfectly still. My left eye is open. I see. Therefore, I must be conscious.

"Are you alright?" Sarner asks again.

"NO! Alright I'm not," I say. "I am one large bruise. I'm in shock."

A young couple, the girl in jeans and a pink halter top, stare at us.

"Would you run to the gate, have them send someone from first aid, or security? My friend is hurt," says Sarner.

"The Powerboarder went that way," the girl says as they hurry off. She has a nasty, nasal Bronx accent. Sarner probes.

"Anything broken?" I ask.

"Only your face as far as I can tell." Sarner blows grit away

86

from in front of my mouth.

"The veteran, Bobby Monday, runs for Wilks as Pokey Valdez the shortstop steps in to bat. Corcoran is obviously shaken up. The umpire has allowed him some warm-up pitches. I imagine the umpires are shaken up, too. I don't know anyone in the game who doesn't like the indestructible Hadrian Wilks."

We can hear the roar of the crowd honouring Hadrian Wilks as the ambulance carries him off the playing field.

A security guard and a young man in a white shirt with a Red Cross arm band hurry toward us. The pool of blood under my head grows larger.

"Can you move?" asks the first aid person. "Should we move him?" he says to Sarner, who has identified himself as a doctor. Sarner nods.

"I can move," I say. With the young man's help Sarner rolls me onto my back, where I lay like a squashed bug.

"We'd better call for an ambulance," the first aid person says to the Security Guard and Sarner.

"Give me a minute," I say. "I'll be able to walk." Wouldn't it be ironic if I ended up in the same vehicle as Hadrian Wilks, I think?

After my brief stint of flying through the air I landed palms first. Both hands are bleeding. The dizziness dissipates. I crawl a few feet to retrieve my glasses, one lens scourged with deep grooves. One of the arms snapped off.

"That eye looks really bad," the first aid person says. "Do you think you can stand up. We could help you to the First Aid Room under the grandstand."

With Sarner on one side, the First Aid person on the other, they manage to get me to my feet.

"I feel a little queasy," I say.

My right eye is already swelling shut.

In the First Aid Room, Sarner stops the blood flow, cleanses the abrasions with antiseptic, recommends that when I feel well enough we should go to the nearest hospital for a tetanus shot, possibly sutures.

Sarner and the first aid people agree that I am in mild shock. "Just lie still for a while, and keep that blanket around you," they say.

We never did get to see the game. Ironically, we waited for hours in the emergency room of the hospital while inside Hadrian Wilks had his wounds cleaned and sutured, and received a tetanus booster.

Several reporters were milling around the Emergency Waiting Room, speculating on how long Hadrian Wilks would be out of action, and if the injury might possibly end his career.

It turned out that I had another fractured cheekbone, with everything on the right side of my face displaced in some manner.

"What about Hadrian Wilks?" I asked a reporter as I was leaving.

"The guy is truly indestructible," the reporter said, shaking his head in wonder. No breaks, just a bruised cheekbone and a one-stitch cut under his eye. No indication of any vision problems. The doctors say he should be able to bat in maybe three days. No reason he can't play a little defence tomorrow. I guess that's today," he added, looking at his watch. "And keep his string intact. Some guys sure have all the luck."

"They sure do," I said. I told him about the incident with the Powerboarder in the parking lot and sustaining a much worse injury to the same part of his face. "Some guys don't have any luck at all," I went on.

I was off work nearly two weeks, had to undergo two

minor surgeries, have a metal pin inserted in my cheekbone. Even after two weeks my eyes were still black and swollen. I looked like I'd gone ten rounds with a promising middleweight.

"Sarner," I asked, "how many injuries have I had in the past fourteen years?"

"More than I want to remember. You, Yossi, are the unluckiest, most accident prone son of a bitch who ever lived."

"Would you guess one a year?" I persisted.

"At least."

"Okay, now listen to this: three weeks ago I fell and broke my cheekbone, got cuts and bruises and scrapes. When was the one before that?"

"Last August, I guess. You were golfing, stepped into a sand trap and broke your right ankle."

"And before that?"

"You fell down coming out of a restaurant. Before that you were playing catch with your son, took one on the right ring finger."

"It'll never be the same."

I waved my right hand in his face. The first joint of the ring finger appeared stiff and permanently swollen.

"Okay, so now we go back two years to the fall at the restaurant. I was talking, wasn't looking where I was going. There was a small step down. I caught myself by grabbing a parked car but I strained a groin muscle. I limped for two months; those kind of injuries never heal."

"What are you getting at?" asked Sarner. "You looking for a pattern?

"Seriously, I think there might be. All my injuries have taken place during baseball season.

10

It is Sarner to whom I first mention the word dybbuk.

"Dybbuk is what?" says Sarner.

"Mythology mainly, touches sometimes religion. A dybbuk, I've heard, is a wandering soul, is someone who takes on the pain of others."

"You think you? All these accidents?"

"Would explain a lot. But I've come up with a theory. Not just in general do I take on pain. Specifically, Hadrian Wilks. Sarner, I've been doing homework. Thousands of sports pages over twenty years. Wilks plays like tomorrow don't exist. He's injured too many times to count, sprains, twists, muscle pulls. Looks bad at the time, a few hours later he's recovered enough to play the next day. Me, I ache. Terminal ache. Wilks is injured, I suffer the pain, the disablement."

"Such a thing I have never heard." We are playing dominoes. We have become friends because of my sprains, my fractures. Twice a week I try to win back some of my money. Sarner is too good for me. He has designed a variation of the game, seven dominoes each. Sarner wins far too often for it to be luck. Thank heaven I am a good accountant, make a fine living.

"You don't know your religion?" I accuse Sarner.

"Who has time for obscurities?"

"I'm making time. I'm on to something. I'm going to take my story to the press, to TV, to magazines. I have proof. I have checked every injury suffered by Hadrian Wilks, and each one corresponds with an accident of mine, an injury, a fall."

"I'd be careful if I were you, Yossi. No good can come from this."

Sarner, as usual, is right.

10

I began to put two and two together and what it added up to was something irregular.

In winter I sometimes resort to teaching a semester of Bonehead Accounting at a community college named for a woman who was murdered by a jealous husband, to students who shouldn't be allowed within five hundred yards of a college unless they're bussing tables in the cafeteria. Time on my hands. I began doing some genuine research.

I spent days in the newspaper morgue reading the sports pages, seeing how many times in his many-season streak Hadrian Wilks had suffered injuries of any kind, but especially injuries that looked like they might cause him to miss a game.

The research took weeks, but what emerged was a definite pattern. Except for years three, six, and nine, there had been at least one, sometimes several injuries to Hadrian Wilks that at first appeared serious but, had faded quickly, almost always within twenty-four hours (except once when he pulled a hamstring just before All-Star break, and managed to be a designated hitter for four games after the break before returning to first base): a bruise, a strain, a slight sprain, a muscle pull, the kind of injuries a veteran like Hadrian Wilks plays through.

It wasn't until Wilks was nearly ten seasons into his Odyssey that the press took any interest. I mean Gehrig's record had stood for over half a century, Ripkin's for seven years, Martinez' for only three. Hadrian played in the shadow of both, not a lot of pressure or press until recently.

I went back to my diaries for that teenage summer when the streak began. It was all girls and cars and my summer job at the bottling plant where my father was a partner. There were days of blank pages. But there it was, my first injury, Wilks' first serious scare. *July 7: Broke my collarbone while goofing around at the park.* My old man was really pissed at me, like I broke it on purpose. I was showing off for some girls by standing on the kid's swings and took a spill.

In spite of my research, the facts I've uncovered, I've been ignored, turned away, spurned, laughed at by everyone from *USA Today* to *The New York Times*, to *Larry King Live.*

"Fanciful," is the kindest critique I've received, that from *Sports Illustrated,* who at least took time to write me a letter. The editor at *SI* was Jewish. *No indication a dybbuk takes on the pain of others,* was scribbled at the bottom.

"Have some imagination," I faxed back. I received no response.

I called Hadrian Wilks' agent. He listened for about thirty seconds and hung up.

I called the editor at *SI,* spent my own money for the call, waited through ten minutes of "Honey", and "Wichita Lineman", while they tried to locate him.

"But there are individuals who take on the pain of others," I cried. I tried to remain rational, not let my voice rise. Don't destroy your credibility, I said under my breath.

"I'm sorry, Mr. Liebowitz, but there's no way to corroborate your thesis.

"But dates coincide . . . the injuries . . . "

"We'd need medical records, which we can't obtain without Mr., ah, Wilks' permission."

Even Geraldo turned me down. "Intriguing", was how they described my proposition in their letter.

"You're crazy," a cheerful production assistant told me, "but not crazy enough. Maybe if you stalked Hadrian Wilks, sent him threatening letters. Hey, you didn't hear it from me. Depends how badly you want on national television."

‌ᴑ

"Harvey? It's Yossi." I am in Los Angeles on business.

"Who else?"

"We need to talk. You understand what's going on with Wilks."

"You are enjoying the convention. Three thousand accountants roaming the streets. I assume all of LAPD is standing by on a polyester alert."

"This is serious."

"So, tell me. Not another accident?"

"You don't believe me?"

"I have an open mind. So, what goes?"

"You haven't heard? His plane's gone down."

"Wilks?"

"Final game before the All-Star break was in Texas. He's supposed to play in the All-Star game in Cincinnati. He begs a pulled muscle. Gets in his private plane for the short hop to Shreveport and home for three days with his family. He ain't got there yet. Twelve hours his plane is missing. Dead probably."

"I'll turn on the news channel. You think maybe this affects you?"

"I am hiding in my hotel room, ordering room service, in case I should be squashed flat by a taxi if I was to cross a street to a restaurant. Or, I might walk into an open man-hole. Have a piano fall on my head."

"But if he's dead, what you have to worry?"

"What if he's not dead? What if multiple injuries?"

"You should be careful," says Sarner.

"Such advice I don't need. I'm in bed. What can happen to me? Bernice is on the phone from Connecticut every ten minutes. I should take the train home, she says. Imagine me on a train. Head-on collision, or jumps the tracks, rolls down an embankment, bursts into flame."

"Keep in touch," says Sarner. "I'd visit longer but I got two engagements in surgery."

I ease out of bed, careful I shouldn't stub my toe. I put on a robe. I think of making coffee. Who wants to be scalded? I sit carefully on the sofa. Turn on the TV with the remote grounded flat on the table; it shouldn't electrocute me.

My worst fears come true. They have found Wilks' plane crashed in a bayou, torn apart by mangrove trees. CNN is everywhere. Probably Ted Turner himself is there. Police cars, ambulances, flashers whirling. He's alive. Multiple injuries, they say. Oy! Burns, perhaps. Flap, flap, comes a medical helicopter to evacuate Wilks to a burn centre, Dallas? did they say, Atlanta? He's on a stretcher. Wrapped like a mummy. They transfer him to a gurney. Runs beside him a paramedic holding an IV. The helicopter swallows him. Flap, flap, and they're off.

"Enough with this dybbuk," I say to the ceiling. I step onto the balcony. The sun shines. From the street thirty-two stories below I can smell flowers, the sweetness of camelias. I clutch the railing, make sure it is well-anchored, check above me in case something might be falling. I breathe in the perfumed air.

A tremor. A tingle in the bottoms of my feet. I grip the railing harder. From a distance comes a rumble, like a huge herd of invisible buffalo charging closer. Earthquake. I freeze. Glancing to the interior, I watch the chandelier swinging my way. The rumble envelops me. The balcony crumbles beneath my feet. I am airborne. Still clutching the railing, I am hurtling toward the camelias. Time changes confuse me. If I live, how many hours before Sarner will be able to reach me?

The First and Last Annual Six Towns Area Old-Timers' Game

It was my daddy, Johnny O'Day, who came up with the idea of an old-timers' baseball game. Daddy, Earl J. Rasmussen, Torval Imsdahl, and Wasyl Lakusta were sitting around the oilcloth-covered kitchen table in our big old house at the end of Nine Pin Road, playing four-handed cribbage, at which my daddy and Earl J. Rasmussen had just skunked the combination of Imsdahl and Lakusta in the final game to win the afternoon thirteen games to twelve, and all four had been sipping on a one-gallon stone crock of good old Heathen's Rapture, or bring-on-blindness, logging-boot-to-the-side-of-the-head homebrew, thoughtfully provided by Wasyl Lakusta, when my daddy stared out the kitchen window, across the snow-covered tundra that was our south field, where the snow was slowly collapsing and the smell of spring was in the air and the pointy brown heads of bulrushes were poking up through the drifts of the nearest slough, just like crocuses would poke out of the nearby hillside in a few weeks, and he scratched his full head of black Irish curls, and I guess thinking of the game he loved and had played every summer of his life until he landed in the Six Towns Area in the midst of the Depression, said, "I think us old-timers should get us together a baseball team."

Earl J. Rasmussen, who lived alone in the hills with about six hundred sheep and claimed that when he had been twenty-five he had been such a good outfielder for his home town of Norseland, Minnesota, that he was offered a tryout with the Washington Senators of the American Baseball League, said he thought my daddy's suggestion was an A-1, first-rate, hot-damn custard of an idea, and went on to say that though he might be on the shady side of forty-five years old at that moment, he bet with a couple of workouts he could patrol the outfield with the best of them, and whack a baseball a fair distance as well.

Earl J. Rasmussen didn't at that moment elaborate on why he had turned down the tryout with the Washington Senators of the American Baseball League. However, my daddy had recounted his version of the story to Mama and me on numerous occasions: the reason Earl J. Rasmussen turned down the tryout with the Washington Senators of the American Baseball League was that the very young Earl J. Rasmussen, living then in Minnesota, and not owning even one sheep, would have had to ride horseback a considerable distance from his home near Norseland, Minnesota, all the way to Minneapolis, Minnesota, where the tryout camp was being held in the stadium of the Minneapolis Millers, a Triple-A baseball team. And my daddy said, Earl J.

Rasmussen's mother wouldn't let him make the trip.

After suggesting the old-timers' game, my daddy then looked across our oilcloth-covered kitchen table at Torval Imsdahl and said, "How about you?" But Torval Imsdahl, who was also on the shady side of forty-five years, squarely built and able to move his big body with the deliberation of a robot, had emigrated to Canada from Norway when he was a young man, and never played baseball, and had only a passing understanding, or misunderstanding, of the game.

"Oh, I forgot," Daddy went on, "the national sport of Norway is pin-the-tail-on-the-lutefisk."

This was a statement, Torval Imsdahl pointed out, that should not be made by someone who wanted to live long and die happy in a community that was populated mainly by Norwegians and hardly any Irishmen, the reason that there were so many Norwegians and so few Irishmen being that most of the Irishmen had died in a potato famine before they ever got to North America.

Torval Imsdahl went on to say that he understood that the national sport of Ireland was potato famine, unless biting the necks off beer bottles could be considered a national sport.

My daddy pointed out that lutefisk, Norway's national dish, was composed of dried herring soaked in lye, lye being something people in North America used as a disinfectant, and that eating herring and lye probably accounted for the fact that Norway's population was rather small, and the reason so many of that small population had emigrated to North America.

Earl J. Rasmussen said that though Norwegians were few in number, they were made strong by eating lutefisk, so strong that one Norwegian could whip ten Irishmen. Norwegians, he said, were stronger than dirt, something he understood composed ninety percent of Ireland's gross national product.

Torval Imsdahl then mentioned that in the 1880s, when the first Norwegians settled at New Oslo, they had to kill someone in order to start a graveyard.

"When you bury a Norwegian you put lots of stones on top of his grave. You have to, or the Norwegian will get up and attend the party after the funeral. A Norwegian hates to miss a party, especially if the only reason to miss the party is that he's dead," said Earl J. Rasmussen.

My daddy, knowing when he was outnumbered, manoeuvred the conversation back to the old-timers' baseball game by asking Torval Imsdahl if he'd be willing to play right field. Torval Imsdahl said he would if Johnny O'Day would promise to play pin-the-tail-on-the-lutefisk at the next Norwegian wedding.

About this time Mama banged down a cup of black coffee in front of each man.

Both Mama and Daddy hailed from South Carolina, and were raised, Daddy said, about one hundred miles apart geographically, but six hundred miles apart socially. They didn't meet until Mama was travelling on a train that went off the track somewhere near Mount Rushmore in South Dakota, and Daddy was one of the gandy dancers who set her train back on the track.

Mama was known for her plainspokenness, and was certainly the practical one in our family. Daddy was the one who always expected everything to turn out the way he thought it should, and was always perplexed and sometimes sorrowful when it didn't. Mama always expected that everything that could go wrong would go wrong. She was seldom disappointed.

Wasyl Lakusta, who farmed by Lily Lake — though Lily

Lake had dried up years before — said he had watched base-ball for donkey's years, and though he'd never played it, thought it was about the simplest game he'd ever seen.

"In the Ukraine," said Wasyl Lakusta, "we were so poor we played soccer with stones the size of your head, instead of a ball. Kicking those stones fifty yards makes good-for-strong feet. One time I kicked one into the crowd, killed the priest, and injured the mayor. That was why I had to emigrate."

"Soccer," Daddy said, "is a game with all the speed and finesse of civil servants working. But, because we're desperate, Wasyl Lakusta will be our centre fielder."

Daddy decided that since he and Earl J. Rasmussen, the Bear Lundquists, and the Bandy Wickers, all hailed from the United States, and since baseball originated in the United States, that the American expatriates would be the core of the old-timers' baseball team.

By adding Torval Imsdahl and Wasyl Lakusta, they would have seven players, and, they all agreed, they would recruit the infamous Flop Skaalrud to play second base, even though he was usually a catcher, because, they all agreed, Flop Skaalrud always brought his own bat with him, and had only to stare at the youngest Chalupa girl, or the second youngest Venusberg Tomchuck girl, both of whom were rumoured to be hot-blooded, for his bat to materialize.

Mama interrupted to say she had definitely heard enough of that smutty kind of talk, but the men didn't pay a lot of attention.

The old-timers felt they held a definite advantage at catcher, and first base, since Bear Lundquist, who was sixty-two years old and arthritic, still caught regularly for the Sangudo Mustangs, and Mrs. Bear Lundquist, who, though she wasn't arthritic, moved like she was, still played first base for the Sangudo Mustangs.

"Yes, sir, you ought to see old Flop wield that weapon," my daddy said.

"Not in front of the boy!" said Mama.

"Never wields it in front of children, Olivia, you should know that," said Daddy, getting a fierce glare from Mama in return.

By his own recollection, my daddy was a mighty fine third baseman, and after the First World War had played some minor league baseball in Florida and California, and South Dakota, though I could never quite pin him down as to where in Florida or California he had played, or who for, or who with, or how long. I had never seen Daddy play baseball, and looked forward to watching him field the hot corner, as he called it, while wondering if he could field as good a game as he talked.

"He was never any better a ball player than he thought he was," Mama said, after I inquired one afternoon as she was darning socks by the light of the south window. "I married your daddy because he was a nice, cheerful man who never expected to bat less than .400, never expected to lose a game, and certainly never expected a Depression, which cost him his business and is the reason we live on this god-forsaken farm at the end of the world."

When Mama was twenty years old, my grandfather decided to settle down and bought himself a permanent position as part owner of a copper mine in Butte, Montana, and decided that if he was going to live there forever he might as well have his family with him.

So Mama gave up her job at a Charleston art gallery on Calhoun Street (not far from the statue of John C. Calhoun, who, she said, was famous for a number of things, the oddest being that he was supposed to be the true father of Abraham Lincoln), and caught a train, which in several days would deliver her to Butte, Montana.

As the train was travelling across South Dakota — where, Mama said, the prairie was like a green ocean in every direction, and where the tall buffalo grass swayed down as the train passed just like wind sweeping over water — the track gave way and the engine plowed off through the tall, green buffalo grass, more or less parallel to the direction it had been running in, until it bogged down with its wheels buried in the prairie. The derailment had been so gentle that most of the passengers didn't realize what had happened, Mama said. The crew was very polite and suggested that the passengers might like to have a picnic out on the sunny prairie while they waited for a repair crew to arrive, and as the passengers sat in little groups on the grass, the white-coated waiters from the dining car passed among them handing out sandwiches and cool drinks.

My daddy was living in South Dakota then, almost in the shadow of Mount Rushmore, playing baseball on weekends and working for the railroad during the week. That's how Daddy wound up on the crew sent to put the train back on the track.

Daddy readily admitted that he didn't know a whole lot about putting a train back on the track, his paramount skills being those of charging in from third base to field bunts bare-handed, and hammering doubles down the right field line about every third time he came to bat, but his eyes sure did recognize a beautiful girl when he saw one, and his ears sure did recognize a South Carolina drawl when he heard one, and by the time the train was back on the track, Daddy had decided to spend the last of his ready cash to buy a one-way ticket from wherever on the plains of South Dakota they were, to Butte, Montana, which he did, and Daddy and Mama were married four months later, and Daddy decided to settle down forever, apprenticing himself to a man who built fine houses for the mine owners, doctors, and lawyers of Butte, Montana.

Fortunately, or unfortunately, Daddy had in his veins what he described as "wandering blood". Three years later, a barnstorming baseball team passed through Butte, a team called Brother Pettigrew's Divine Light Baseball Mission, which combined, Brother Pettigrew said, the two Gods of rural North America: the mysterious and sometimes troubling one in the sky and the one of baseball. The team's third baseman was arrested for disturbing the peace in Butte, on account of him kicking out the window of his hotel room at 3 AM and singing "Amazing Grace" in an off-key but very loud voice, a charge that would have gotten him nothing but a two-dollar fine and a lecture, except an eagle-eyed deputy leafed through a stack of "wanted" posters and discovered that the third baseman was wanted in Orlando, Florida, for bank robbery and assault with a deadly weapon, which, my daddy said, could well have been his loud, off-key singing voice.

My daddy was called in to repair the splintered window sash, and next afternoon found himself touring with Brother Pettigrew's Divine Light Baseball Mission.

The team travelled in a circle through Washington, Oregon, and Idaho, then moved up into Canada. They played in Medicine Hat, Alberta; they played in Lethbridge; they played in Calgary; they played in Red Deer; they played in Edmonton — well, not exactly played in Edmonton. There had been a slight misunderstanding, and they had been booked into a softball park and scheduled against a women's softball team. They agreed to make certain adjustments and play the game anyway, but only eleven spectators showed up and the game was canceled. The bus wouldn't start, so the players and Brother Pettigrew had to take a streetcar to their hotel, and when they got up in the morning they discovered that Brother Pettigrew had absconded, owing each and every one of them a full two months' wages. To add insult to injury, though it was barely Labour Day, three inches of wet snow had fallen during the night.

My daddy used the last of his money to send for my mother, and after a string of odd jobs, and building some fine houses, the Depression settled in and they settled on the farm we live on, outside of a town called Fark, sixty miles more or less west of Edmonton, the capital of Alberta. Fark, at the time, consisted of a general store, a community hall, and an empty gas pump. Mama said it was a cruel punishment for anyone to have to live near a town with a name that sounded like a curse word.

"If we are going to have a decent old-timers' club we are going to need a pitcher," said Earl J. Rasmussen.

They racked their brains, while they ignored their coffee and the jug of Heathen's Rapture passed twice around the table; they were unable to name anyone in the Six Towns Area, over thirty-five, who could pitch.

"Pitching is everything," Daddy said. "We'll be playing the young men of the community, and these young fellows stand up at the plate expecting fastballs, knowing they'll hit a fair portion of them halfway to the Edmonton-Jasper Highway. We need somebody with finesse, a guy who can throw off-speed stuff, slow curves that will make his slow fastball look fast. These young fastball hitters would break their backs trying to hit a pitcher like that, if we had one."

"Eddie Grassfires," I said, from my hiding place where I was cuddled up between the woodbox and the kitchen stove.

"Eddie Grassfires? That skinny little Indian?" said Daddy.

"His only saving grace is a passable pickoff move to first

base," objected Earl J. Rasmussen.

"But he's old enough," said Daddy.

"And his fastball is slow enough," agreed Earl J. Rasmussen.

"Do you think we can teach him to throw off-speed?" asked my daddy.

"You could have him practise by throwing soccer-ball-sized rocks," said Wasyl Lakusta. "Would slow him down for sure."

"Wasyl here has played that stone soccer ball off his head one too many times," said Earl J. Rasmussen.

My rabbit-snaring buddy Floyd Wicker's daddy, Bandy Wicker, agreed to play for the old-timers. Unfortunately for the team, even though he hailed from Odessa, Texas, Bandy Wicker had never played baseball.

My daddy, when he found out, said he guessed it was because there was a greater opportunity to get seriously injured while playing football, which Bandy Wicker had done, being a punt return man for his high-school team. And since Bandy Wicker, besides being accident prone, had never weighed more than 120 pounds in his life, he had, while attempting to return punts, on separate occasions broken his left leg, his right arm, and several fingers, as well as having his nose moved dramatically toward the left side of his face.

Under the influence of Heathen's Rapture, or good old bring-on-blindness, logging-boot-to-the-side-of-the-head homebrew, the men gathered around our oilcloth-covered kitchen table in the house at the end of Nine Pin Road agreed that the first practice for the old-timers' baseball team would be held in our south field the first day that

Jamie O'Day Creek, named by my daddy in honour of me, receded sufficiently after the spring flood to make Nine Pin Road passable.

That decision was their first mistake, for our south field, though it looked pretty level in March when it was covered by several feet of just-about-to-melt snow, was not level at all when viewed close up and had an inordinate number of rocks everywhere, along with an inordinate number of low spots that retained water, cleverly hidden beneath bright green grass sprinkled with yellow cowslips.

The lineup for the old-timers' baseball team was: Catcher, Bear Lundquist, who was sixty-two years old and arthritic; First Base, Mrs. Bear Lundquist, who wasn't arthritic but moved like she was; Second Base, the infamous Flop Skaalrud, who, my daddy said, always brought his own bat with him and simply had to stare at the second youngest Venusberg Tomchuck girl for it to materialize; Third Base, my daddy, Johnny O'Day; Shortstop, the accident-prone and frequently injured Bandy Wicker from Odessa, Texas; Right Field, Torval Imsdahl, who, my daddy said, would rather be playing pin-the-tail-on-the-lutefisk; Centre Field, Wasyl "Stone Kicker" Lakusta; Left Field, Earl J. Rasmussen, who lived alone in the hills with about 600 sheep; Pitcher, Eddie Grassfires, who hailed from the big reserve over by Lac Ste. Anne, and who may or may not have known or noticed that Mrs. Edytha Rasmussen Bozniak's ten-year-old daughter, Velvet Bozniak, bore him a striking resemblance.

There is quite a story, one I'm not supposed to know because of my tender age, concerning Eddie Grassfires and Mrs. Edytha Rasmussen Bozniak, at a time when she was still Miss Edytha Rasmussen. Eddie Grassfires worked one summer coiling hay on the Rasmussen farm, and reportedly became enamoured with the young Edytha when she brought cold jugs of ice water to the hayers. So enamored that he would tether his pony in an adjacent field and pay a visit to Edytha's room in the dead of many a summer night. When, as my daddy said, Edytha Rasmussen took something seriously that was poked at her in fun, she eventually confessed her problem to her parents who promptly arranged for her to take a job as a domestic in the city of Edmonton, but the Rasmussens being more imaginative than most, immediately created a beau, a full-scholarshipped orphaned genius named Arthur Bozniak, who was studying electrical engineering at the University of Alberta. There was a wedding, and after a respectable interval a baby girl, Velvet Rasmussen Bozniak, was born, all the while no one in the Six Towns Area ever setting eyes on the full-scholarshipped orphaned genius son-in-law. What would have happened is anybody's guess, but the Rasmussens were rescued by the unanticipated beginning of World War Two, where Arthur Bozniak was one of the first volunteers, and one of the first causalities of the conflict. While everyone in the Six Towns Area knows this story, no one ever lets on to the Rasmussens, particularly Mrs. Edytha Rasmussen Bozniak and her daughter Velvet Rasmussen Bozniak. My mama often says something to the effect that a lifetime of smirking behind your hand is worth far more than a few seconds of triumph.

The first practice was more or less a disaster.

"Considerably more than less," Mama said, after the team clomped into her kitchen in our big log house at the end of Nine Pin Road, tracking all sorts of mud and corruption after them.

Our south field, though it looked wonderful of a sunny Sunday afternoon, with the crocuses flowering in the high spots, and buttercups and cowslips in the low places, turned out to be, to say the least, unkind to baseball players. First off, nothing was level. When they finally did settle on a pitcher's mound, it was about fifteen feet higher than home plate, which meant that first and third bases were also much higher than home plate and second base was just barely visible to Bear Lundquist when he was standing, and not at all when he was in his crouch, which once he got into he found really hard to get out of because of his being arthritic.

The outfield was another problem: first off, none of the outfielders could see home plate, so anything hit beyond second base came as a complete surprise, and secondly, though from a distance the outfield looked like one of those advertisements picturing what heaven should look like — green, green grass sprinkled with colourful wildflowers — in reality, underneath the green, green grass was a certain amount of moisture, meaning that in left field Earl J. Rasmussen got to stand in sticky mud, and in centre field Wasyl Lakusta was wading in two inches of water, while in right field Torval Imsdahl had to put on his fishing boots because the slough water rode calf-high all afternoon.

Flop Skaalrud and Bandy Wicker ran into each other trying to field a ground ball over second base and Bandy Wicker sprained his ankle and couldn't play the rest of the afternoon, which he spent sitting alongside third base taking an occasional swig from a stone crock of good old Heathen's Rapture, bring-on-blindness, logging-boot-to-the-side-of-the-head homebrew.

To top things off, in spite of several reminders, Eddie Grassfires didn't show up to practise his pitching, so with Bandy Wicker's injury the team was two players short, plus somebody had to hit baseballs into the field.

I filled in at second base, where I could occasionally stop

a ground ball, although I didn't have enough arm to throw to first. After a lot of wheedling from Daddy, Mama filled in for Eddie Grassfires, Mama holding the ball above her head like a trophy, then whirling her pitching arm in circles like she was maybe screwing a corkscrew into an invisible cork, then letting the ball fly somewhere in the general direction of the plate, where Daddy, having left third base vacant, would try to hit the ball to one of the old-timers.

Just as the sun was thinking about setting and everybody was about to go home, Eddie Grassfires, being, my daddy said, on Indian time, showed up for the practice, but by that time the three baseballs that had been used that afternoon were being dried out in our oven, as were the shoes of most of the genuine players and both of the conscripted players (Mama and me).

The old-timers decided that their next practice would be held at the Fark Baseball Grounds, where, Bandy Wicker said, at least the catcher could see second base when the weather was clear.

At that practice, a few of the young ballplayers, including Truckbox Al McClintock, came by to watch and snicker, as it became clear that even on a regulation baseball field, perhaps especially on a regulation field, the old-timers were not going to strike fear into the hearts of any genuine baseball team, or even just a collection of young, local baseball players with less than a minimum of talent.

The young ballplayers decided they didn't want to play the old-timers, even in a five-inning exhibition game, because as far as they could see they had everything to lose and nothing to gain. If they won, it would simply be young players beating a bunch of old men, as they would be expected to do, while if they lost, they would look foolish.

At the pronouncement of the young ballplayers, everybody except possibly my daddy and Earl J. Rasmussen, breathed a sigh of relief. In spite of the old-timers offering to put up twenty dollars if the young ballplayers would do the same, winner take all, the whole project engendered about as much excitement as a Santa Claus suit in July, and the old-timers' game would have died a peaceful death, except that in what appeared to be an unrelated matter, Bear Lundquist set a few wheels in motion by writing to his brother-in-law in Calgary describing young Truckbox Al McClintock's baseball-playing prowess, and those wheels in motion eventually resulted in a long distance telephone call from John "The Raja of Renfrew" Ducey, advising Truckbox Al McClintock that he had been selected to play in an exhibition game at Renfrew Park, down on the river flats, in Edmonton, Alberta, for the unimaginatively named Alberta All-Stars against a team of major leaguers in their prime, featuring such names as Bob Feller, Hal Newhouser and Joe DiMaggio himself.

That unexpected development, Daddy said, opened a whole new can of worms, because even though everyone from the Six Towns Area was poor, and it was alright for them to be poor, and it was alright for them to look and act poor if they travelled, say, to the city of Edmonton, but it wasn't alright for one of their children to look and act poor if he, say, travelled to the city of Edmonton, as Truckbox Al McClintock had been summoned to do.

After a quick meeting of the old-timers it was agreed that if an old-timers' game was properly managed financially — and Earl J. Rasmussen volunteered to be financial manager — such a game could raise enough money to buy Truckbox Al McClintock a brand-new baseball uniform. Since there was now a goal, the young baseball players would not only look like cowards, they would look like jealous cowards if they refused to participate, Daddy said.

However, the old-timers didn't want to go too far with their philanthropy, Daddy said, because if they did, they might wound the McClintock pride, which was known to be considerable. And Curly McClintock, Truckbox Al's father, had already let it be known that he was going to manage somehow to get Truckbox Al a new pair of baseball spikes, size thirteen, as well as a new baseball glove.

My daddy, Earl J. Rasmussen and Bandy Wicker (though Bandy Wicker had never played baseball) did their best to teach Eddie Grassfires (when they could convince Eddie Grassfires to come to a practice) to throw off-speed pitches so that his slow fastball would look faster in comparison.

Once, the whole team went to the reserve at Lac Ste. Anne, riding in the back of Curly McClintock's dump truck, Lac Ste. Anne being farther east than people from the Six Towns Area usually went, tracked Eddie Grassfires down in the Lac Ste. Anne Hotel bar, and made him practise throwing off-speed pitches for close to three-quarters of an hour.

The old-timers' game was set for the New Oslo baseball grounds of a Sunday afternoon. Unfortunately, on the Saturday night preceding that Sunday, there was a severe four-hour fry-the-cottonwoods, electrocute-your-cattle thunder and lightning storm, as Daddy called it, so the field was in about the same condition as our south pasture had been for the first practice.

The turnout for the old-timers' game was the largest since the box social two years previous after the Lute Magnussens had been burned out of a cold December. Earl J. Rasmussen dutifully collected twenty-five cents from each adult and ten cents from each child, and calculated that there would be just enough to buy Truckbox Al McClintock a brand new baseball uniform at wholesale prices, with enough left over to put a down payment on a purebred ewe he had had his eye on at a sheep farm over west of Sangudo.

What kind of baseball uniform to buy precipitated a meeting of the Farmers' Union in our seldom-used living room at the end of Nine Pin Road. Bear Lundquist, who had always been partial to the Chicago Cubs, said there was no question but what the boy should be decked out in a Chicago Cub uniform. My daddy pointed out logically that since it was the genuine St. Louis Cardinals of the National Baseball League who had shown an implied interest in Truckbox Al McClintock, he should be dressed in a St. Louis Cardinal uniform.

Bandy Wicker said that though football was his game, he had always been partial to the New York Yankees and since Truckbox Al McClintock, from all reports, was going to be the next Babe Ruth, the boy should be decked out in Yankee pinstripes on the day when he was getting his big break.

Earl J. Rasmussen said that he had always been a Detroit Tiger fan, and since it had been his idea to raise the money, the least everyone could do would be to allow him to choose what type of uniform it should be.

My daddy pointed out that if all went well, Earl J. Rasmussen was going to be able to buy himself a championship ewe with the remaining money from the old-timers' game, and that a purebred ewe should be sufficient reward in itself, and Earl J. Rasmussen shouldn't be so greedy as to want the boy to wear a Detroit Tiger uniform when Earl J. was already being amply compensated.

After two stone crocks' worth of discussion, and after the discussion almost turned into a shoving match on a couple of occasions, but never quite developed into a fistfight, alter-cation, or genuine brouhaha, the final decision was left with Truckbox Al McClintock's daddy, Curly McClintock, who would be the one to buy the uniform at Marshall-Wells Wholesale in Edmonton.

The problem concerning what uniform Truckbox Al McClintock should wear on the day he was getting his big baseball break, as most problems do if left alone, resolved itself, for when Curly McClintock got to Marshall-Wells Wholesale on 104th Street in Edmonton, he found they only stocked two types of baseball uniforms: whitish flannels for home team uniforms, and greyish flannels for visiting team uniforms. None of the uniforms had any team crests on them, and if he wanted to order a team crest it would take at least three months, that is, if it didn't get lost in the mail coming from Louisville, Kentucky, or wherever it was those kind of exotic baseball products came from.

Since the unimaginatively named Alberta All-Stars would be the home team, Curly McClintock decided on white flan-nels, size forty-two short, for his son, Truckbox Al.

As scheduled, the old-timers' game got all set to go on the very muddy New Oslo baseball grounds. Almost everybody in the Six Towns Area was there, including Loretta Cake, who lived in an abandoned cabin about a mile from Doreen Beach and cohabitated with about one hundred cats.

Sven Bjornsen, of Bjornsen Bros. Swinging Cowboy Musicmakers, donned his umpire's mask and shouted "Play ball."

From that point on, the game went downhill to a certain extent.

In spite of not practising very much, Eddie Grassfires learned his lessons well, for instead of throwing the ball toward the plate as hard as he could, with the young, anxious, muscular batters knowing he was throwing as hard as he could, and knowing that if they swung hard they would connect with a certain percentage of his pitches, enough to make him the losing pitcher almost as many times as he was the starting pitcher, Eddie Grassfires threw the off-speed pitches my daddy had taught him.

He threw something that today would be called a knuckleball, holding the ball by bracing the first two joints of his middle and index fingers against the seams, making the ball jump and tremble as it lurched toward the plate, where the young, anxious, muscular batters, used to hitting fastballs, broke their backs swinging at it. He also threw a slow curve that was seldom in the strike zone, but looked so tantalizing that the young, anxious, muscular batters swatted at it anyway. He also threw his fastball, but mixed in with the slow pitches, his fastball, though it was slow, looked fast, and the young, anxious, muscular batters tended to get out in front of it and slash it foul.

In the top of the fifth and final inning the New Oslo Blue Devils, as the old-timers' opponents chose to call themselves since they were playing in New Oslo though all the teams in the Six Towns Area were represented on their squad, scored two runs to tie the game. Eddie Grassfires looked as though he was lobbing basketballs to the plate; one of the Dwerynchuck twins singled, and Truckbox Al McClintock hit the first pitch a good twenty yards beyond the mowed area in centre field, beyond the slough grass and water and directly into a blueberry muskeg, where Wasyl Lakusta, the centre fielder, stopped to pick and eat a couple of handfuls of blueberries before tossing the badly-stained baseball back to the infield.

It was agreed that if the game remained tied through five innings, no extra innings would be played. Earl J. Rasmussen led off the bottom of the fifth with a double. Slow Andy McMahon, who was the only replacement available after the injury-prone Bandy Wicker slid headfirst into the shin guard of the New Oslo catcher in the fourth inning, breaking his nose in one and possibly two places, waddled into the batter's box, all four hundred pounds of him drooping and sagging and languishing in several directions at once.

"Get hit by a pitch!" was my daddy's advice to Slow Andy McMahon. But Slow Andy held his bat high and stared out at the pitcher over his inflated cheeks, sagging jowls, and numerous double chins. He didn't see the first pitch which was a strike. He didn't see the second pitch either, but it hit his bat and trickled toward second base. Slow Andy was still mulling over the idea of laying down his bat and streaking toward first base when he was thrown out at first, but on the play, Earl J. Rasmussen easily advanced to third.

The old-timers had a man on third and one out, with my daddy coming to the plate. Daddy had already had two hits, and the New Oslo outfielders, known for the strength but not the accuracy of their throwing arms, made it almost certain that a fly ball of any kind would score the winning run.

The first pitch to Daddy was high and outside. For reasons known only to him, as the catcher lobbed the ball back to the pitcher, Earl J. Rasmussen decided to steal home.

Earl J. broke from third base, streaking toward home with, as my daddy would say later, all the speed of waste passing through a long dog. Daddy only said waste when Mama was within earshot. The pitcher caught the movement of Earl J. Rasmussen out of the corner of his eye, and as soon as the lobbed ball reached his glove, he fired it back toward home plate.

My daddy, standing peacefully in the left-handed batter's box, saw that Earl J. was going to be out by about thirty feet, so he exercised what he later said was his inborn baseball instinct and stepped into the pitch, slamming it deep into the gap in left centre field, the ball landing with a thunk at about the time Earl J. Rasmussen slid across home plate.

Nobody seemed too sure of what was going on, for my daddy didn't run toward first base. He just stood peacefully in the left-handed batter's box, grinning what Earl J. Rasmussen would later describe as the grin of an egg-sucking dog, while the entire New Oslo Blue Devils baseball team began a charge toward home plate, each and every Blue Devil mouth screaming in outrage, affront, despair, and pure bafflement.

Umpire Sven Bjornsen, of the Bjornsen Bros. Swinging Cowboy Musicmakers, first raised his arms to call time, then raised his right arm into Daddy's face and declared him out for interference, a gesture that eased the volume of outrage and affront, though only temporarily.

Sven Bjornsen then pointed at Earl J. Rasmussen, indicating that the run did not count and gesturing decisively to signal that Earl J. Rasmussen had to go back to third base.

At that gesture, the screams of outrage, affront, despair and pure bafflement rose to a crescendo that caused about fifteen crows to rise in the air from a cottonwood tree next to the hot dog stand. The gist of the New Oslo Blue Devils' argument was that Earl J. Rasmussen should also be out.

"Not so," said Umpire Sven Bjornsen. The ball was dead at the point Johnny O'Day interfered with the play; my daddy was out, and everything went back to the way it was before he interfered with the ball.

"But Earl J. Rasmussen was going to be out by thirty feet," the New Oslo Blue Devils screamed in outrage, affront, despair, and pure bafflement.

"The play never took place," Umpire Sven Bjornsen

argued logically. "Who was to say the catcher was going to hold onto the ball, and what if Earl J. had changed his direction and gotten safely back to third?"

"But," the New Oslo Blue Devils screamed, "a team shouldn't be able to profit from wrongdoing. If Johnny O'Day hadn't interfered with the ball, Earl J. Rasmussen would have been out and the old-timers would have had two out and nobody on base. But, because Johnny O'Day interfered with the ball the old-timers have a man on third and two out. They have profited from wrongdoing."

Umpire Sven Bjornsen and the captain of the New Oslo Blue Devils resorted to perusing *The Baseball Rule Book*; unfortunately, the only copy available in the Six Towns Area had eleven or twelve pages missing, and if there was anything in *The Baseball Rule Book* that covered the situation, and there probably was, no one could find it. Umpire Sven Bjornsen quoted from a Jimmie Rodgers song that he and the Bjornsen Bros. Swinging Cowboy Musicmakers played and sang at box socials, whist drives, sports days, community dances and ethnic weddings — "They say the good must suffer for other people's sins, but there is a crown awaiting where a new life begins."

The quotation caused the New Oslo Blue Devils to scream with even more outrage, affront, despair, and pure bafflement than ever before.

All the while my daddy stood peacefully in the left handed batter's box, grinning what Earl J. Rasmussen would later describe as the grin of an egg-sucking dog.

When the brouhaha had finally subsided, the next batter, Wasyl Lakusta, swung very late at a fastball and hit a little bleeder to right field, where it dropped halfway between the right fielder and the first baseman, Earl J. Rasmussen trotting home with the winning run in what proved to be the first and last annual Six Towns Area Old-Timers' Baseball Game.

As the crowd was dispersing, the winning pitcher, Eddie Grassfires, turned around from his seat on the bench along the third-base line to face the fans on the small bleacher directly behind him; two of the fans on the small bleacher were Mrs. Edytha Rasmussen Bozniak and her daughter, Velvet Bozniak.

Eddie Grassfires nodded hello to Mrs. Edytha Rasmussen Bozniak, who nodded hello to Eddie Grassfires. Seeing Eddie Grassfires, that skinny Indian pitcher whose only saving grace was a passable pickoff move to first base, face-to-face with Velvet Bozniak, it became apparent that if Eddie Grassfires was to place a Christmas-red velvet bow behind each ear and attach a Christmas-red velvet bow at the throat of his uniform the way Velvet Bozniak had a Christmas-red bow behind each ear and at the throat of her blouse, why they would not only look like they resembled each other, they'd look like genuine close relatives. On second glance, it became apparent that even without Eddie Grassfires wearing any Christmas-red velvet bows, they looked like genuine close relatives.

"You got a pretty little girl there, Edytha," said Eddie Grassfires.

"She is, isn't she?" said Mrs. Edytha Rasmussen Bozniak.

"I was sorry to hear you lost your husband in the war," said Eddie Grassfires.

"Thank you," said Mrs. Edytha Rasmussen Bozniak.

My daddy wondered aloud on the drive home from the first and last annual Six Towns Area Old-timers' Baseball Game if, while Eddie Grassfires and Mrs. Edytha Rasmussen Bozniak were saying those things by way of conversation, they were both thinking of the summer nights when Eddie tethered his pony to graze in a meadow on Anker Rasmussen's farm and made his way up to the Rasmussen house, where Edytha was waiting for him?

He also wondered aloud if, when Velvet Bozniak looked into the face of Eddie Grassfires, she didn't see her own face looking back at her, just like she was staring into a magic mirror of some kind.

"My daddy died a hero in the war," Velvet Bozniak had said to Eddie Grassfires, staring into his face, which was a strange, distorted reflection of her own.

"You should be proud of him," Eddie Grassfires said.

"I am," said Velvet Bozniak, who, as she had done before and would do all her life, never let anything people said or do bother her a whole lot.

Even though Truckbox Al McClintock had his tryout in a brand-new white flannel uniform, he never did become the next Babe Ruth. But Velvet Bozniak moved to the city of Edmonton when she was about eighteen, the very year that television arrived in the city of Edmonton, and Velvet Bozniak went to work for Edmonton's one and only TV station. She later moved on to Toronto, then to Los Angeles, and finally to New York — if you look at the closing credits of the evening news broadcast on one of the major TV networks, you'll see Velvet Bozniak's name listed as one of the producers. So in the long run, with the unacknowledged help of Eddie Grassfires, the Six Towns Area did produce a celebrity, even if it wasn't a baseball player. And it was six weeks before Daddy stopped grinning like an old egg-sucking dog.

The Lime Tree

It didn't surprise Fitz that McGarrigle, even though at seventy-eight he was a year younger than Fitz, was beginning to lose it. Yes, Fitz decided, carrying on conversations in the courtyard with long-dead relatives was a definite sign. McGarrigle was out there now, crouched by the lime tree, even though it was well after midnight. Though both men were used to turning off the TV after the ten o'clock news, and heading for bed, they had become positively nocturnal in the past few weeks, McGarrigle out in a corner of the moon-blue courtyard talking to his dead wife and daughter, Fitz pacing, worrying, keeping an eye on McGarrigle.

"A couple of old women." That was how Fitz had heard himself and McGarrigle described by a young man in their apartment complex, Lime Tree Courts. McGarrigle had just passed by the pool, limping in from the parking lot, a sack of groceries in the crook of his left arm, his rubber-tipped cane helping him keep his balance.

"Queer as three-dollar bills," another young man, dangling his feet in the azure-blue water of the swimming pool, had added.

"I heard they were both football players about a hundred years ago," the first young man said. The speakers didn't realize that Fitz was standing on his balcony two floors above the pool. Voices travelled clearly through the dry, early evening air.

"They're not queer, at least in the way you mean it," a girl in an orange bikini contributed. "They're just old. I talked to them once. They both had wives and families. And it was baseball they played, though you're right it must have been a hundred years ago."

The group around the pool all laughed.

Fitz didn't hear any more because McGarrigle was thumping at the apartment door, probably having misplaced his keys again. They should have seen us in our prime, Fitz thought. We could have licked the whole lot of them, their friends and relatives, and the box they came in. Bull McGarrigle was like a raging bull in them days, alright. Saw him almost single-handedly whip six Boston Red Sox in a barroom brawl after a Saturday doubleheader. "Them Red Sox always choke in the clutch," McGarrigle wheezed as he and Fitz walked away from the bar, McGarrigle shaking beer and blood and broken glass off himself like a wet dog emerging from a river.

He's always been larger than life, Fitz thought, and he fumbled the door open. "What took you so long? Tangled up in yer knitting yarn again, Granny," said McGarrigle, ducking his head, crowding into the apartment like an oversized sofa.

Though pushing eighty, Fitz held himself ramrod

straight. He walked slowly, his full head of porcelain-white hair contrasting his healthy pink complexion. His eyes were a clear, aquamarine colour. He did not wear glasses or a hearing aid. McGarrigle, on the other had, looked every bit of his seventy-eight years. He had taken on a bulldogish appearance in his later years, his large ears emphasizing the huge size of his head, his potato-like face blotched and mottled. His huge catcher's hands were gnarled and arthritic. He walked with his legs spread wide, guided by a redwood walking stick.

10

Lime Tree Courts consisted of seventy apartments built around a swimming pool and shrub garden. Most of the units were studios and one-bedrooms. Fitz and McGarrigle shared one of the only two-bedroom units.

Fitz had been widowed most recently. Pegeen had been gone seven years. At first he'd puttered around the big house in Gardena, taking little pleasure from the landscaping and house repairs that seemed to occupy most of his time. He and McGarrigle golfed year round and had season tickets to California Angels' games. When the Angels were on the road they often drove to Chavez Ravine in McGarrigle's little Buick, to watch the Dodgers.

McGarrigle's wife, Mary-Kaye, had been dead for almost twelve years. Their marriage had not been as happy as Fitz and Pegeen's. Neither McGarrigle nor Mary-Kaye had ever been the same after they'd lost their daughter.

Fitz and McGarrigle talked of moving to one or the other's house; McGarrigle's was grander, with an ocean view, and he could afford to hire a gardener and a part-time maid. Eventually, the empty space became too much for McGarrigle, even with the thought of company. So both houses were sold, and together Fitz and McGarrigle bought a unit in a new and luxurious singles complex, Lime Tree Courts.

Neither would have admitted it publicly, but what prompted their particular purchase was what Fitz had heard referred to as the vanity of the athlete, the hubris that kept thirty-five-year-old pitchers, hitters, quarterbacks, and tennis players hacking away long after their bodies had ceased to react promptly to the commands of their brain.

Fitz and McGarrigle each harboured a secret fantasy that a young woman in Lime Tree Courts would find them attractive. That a young Pegeen or Mary-Kaye would see through the erosion of time to the magnificence that had been, and each harboured an even more forlorn hope that the young woman's youth would somehow transform them, even for a short time, into what they had once been.

○

Friends for almost sixty years — McGarrigle from New York City, Fitz (Elwood Joseph Fitzgerald on formal occasions) from a Kansas farm — they'd met playing baseball in Louisville in the first years of the Great Depression. Both had up and down careers in the Bigs, McGarrigle catching for the Browns and the Senators, Fitz playing second base and shortstop for five clubs, with a few stops in the minors in between. His longest stint was a full season at second base for the Pirates in 1933. Fitz had played part of twelve seasons, and he was quick to point out to McGarrigle that his career had been longer, even if he hadn't played as many games.

"I was still turning the double play when you were hammering 2x4s in California," Fitz would crow.

After baseball, McGarrigle started a construction company in Los Angeles; he cashed in on the post-second-world-war building boom, moved later to apartment construction during which time his company had built several complexes similar to Lime Tree Courts.

Fitz and Pegeen had settled briefly in St. Louis, until at McGarrigle's insistence they visited California, and again at McGarrigle's insistence, stayed.

McGarrigle offered to take Fitz into the construction business. "I don't have the temperament to be a boss," Fitz said. "I like to leave my job behind at the end of the day and head home to Pegeen and the kids."

McGarrigle found Fitz a job as a representative for a large building supply firm.

Fitz never regretted his choice. He and Pegeen had four children, two boys, two girls, all settled now. There were grandchildren galore and by the size and beauty of a couple of his teenage granddaughters, he guessed he might live to be a great-grandfather.

McGarrigle had not been so fortunate. His marriage to Mary-Kaye was good enough; they both enjoyed fighting, one minute flinging plates and curses at one another, the next making up, putting the same amount of passion into reconciliation.

"Don't you try any of that aggressive behaviour with me," Fitz told McGarrigle when they made the final decision to move in together, "or, by God, I'll pin your ears back like Mary-Kaye could never do."

Mary-Kaye and McGarrigle had had one daughter, Maggie, as beautiful and sweet-tempered a girl as ever lived. In her senior year of high school, as she was riding her bicycle to a babysitting job a few blocks from her home, she'd turned to wave to a friend and steered her bike into the side of a passing car. One second she was alive, the next dead.

McGarrigle muddled through. Mary-Kaye didn't. She

became at first a secret, and later a not-so-secret drinker. She withdrew from everyone, including McGarrigle, refused help, and McGarrigle spent the last fifteen years of her life, essentially alone.

🔾

It was his long lost daughter, Maggie, McGarrigle was talking with now, out under the lime tree in the dew-fresh hours before dawn.

"We have such a lot to catch up on, Fitz," McGarrigle had said, after the first episode, a week ago.

Neither man had ever been nocturnal, so Fitz, when he'd heard the outside door latch snap at 4:00 AM had gotten up to investigate. He'd caught McGarrigle, not going out but coming in, shoes in hand, like a guilty husband.

"Let me guess," said Fitz. "It's one of the flight attendants in #27B. I noticed the one with green eyes staring at you last week."

"It's my cane that enthrals them," said McGarrigle. "None of these sweet young things have ever dated a man with a cane. Of course, the symbolism of the cane doesn't escape them either."

"Could I interest you in telling me the truth?" Fitz said. "I gather you've been outdoors for some time. You've got the cool smell of the night on you, and your shirt is wilted."

"I believe I'd rather lie," said McGarrigle.

"At least give me a hint," said Fitz. "You're not one to miss your sleep without good reason. Is it animal, vegetable, or mineral?"

"Eternal," said McGarrigle.

"You're having an experience with *Himself?*" said Fitz, nodding toward the ceiling. Neither he nor McGarrigle were of a spiritual nature.

"Not so you'd recognize," said McGarrigle. "What's happened to me is my fondest dream come true. It's what I've wished for in my heart every moment of the last twenty-seven years. Out there, under the lime tree, I've been talking with Maggie."

"To your Maggie?"

What with all the publicity given to Altzheimer's Disease, both Fitz and McGarrigle kept a wary eye on each other, kidding each other about Oldtimer's Disease when they forgot names, put their eyeglasses in the refrigerator, or walked about with their zippers undone.

"Just trolling," McGarrigle would say, zipping his fly, but every joke was tinged with worry.

"Yes, my Maggie," McGarrigle said, after a pause, while he gazed around the living room as if trying to remember where he was.

"What did she have to say?"

"She relieved me of my fear of death. Not that I had a great fear."

"I see," said Fitz. "And Maggie, is she still a girl, or is she a middle-aged lady?"

"Well, now, I didn't ask. Her voice is as I remember it though. Sweet, and with a little catch just before she laughs."

"So why here? Why now? Why you? You're not the only old ballplayer hungry for loved ones lost. What did you do that no one else has done? Do you belong to the right organization? Did you give to the right charity?"

McGarrigle looked startled, as if he'd just been awakened.

"It's way past my bedtime, Fitz. Yours, too. It's the lime tree, Maggie told me, the way it scents the air, it . . . " McGarrigle tottered off toward his bedroom leaving his statement unfinished.

10

So it had been for several nights: McGarrigle pacing the living room, clock-watching, waiting for midnight, waiting for the pool lights to go out, waiting for the last stragglers to leave the poolside area.

"I want to spend every precious moment I can with her, Fitz. She says she doesn't know how long she'll be able to come to me."

Was McGarrigle really losing it? Fitz wondered. Was it possible to appear coherent in most respects, yet be loony as a bedbug? Fitz sat alone in the living room for a long time. "You're not the only one has lost someone you loved," he said, rising slowly, the low-slung sofa taking its usual toll on his back, and heading outdoors.

Fitz padded slowly around the pool and, ducking his head, walked the concrete block path through oleander, bougainvillea, what may have been hibiscus, past orange trees, a lacy-leafed olive tree, until he came to, off in a corner next to the concrete-block wall, a lime tree.

The earth was dry, even dusty. Lovers walked to the end of the sidewalk and turned around. As Fitz left the sidewalk, a few fallen leaves crisped under foot.

Soon after he and McGarrigle had moved into Lime Tree Courts, they had explored the outback, as McGarrigle had called it.

What had drawn McGarrigle out here in the dead of night to this isolated corner, to this small lime tree?

Fitz remembered as a boy in Kansas planting an orange seed in a soup can full of dirt, watching the plant grow day by day, being amazed when his mother squeezed the small deep-green leaves, unleashing the heavenly scent of oranges in the middle of winter.

Fitz pressed gently on a leaf of the lime tree, inhaled the pure perfume it emitted fresh as a dash of cold water, obliterating the exhaust fumes, seeming to quell the sound of traffic from nearby streets.

"Oh, Maggie, I hope you're here, dear," Fitz whispered. "I hope you're talking with your daddy, that it's not just old age, a failing mind and terminal wishful thinking he's suffering from."

꒰০

Another evening, as they waited, Fitz kept pressing McGarrigle for details: Did he see Maggie? If so, did he touch her? If he touched her, was she there in reality, or just a shade?

"Fitz, do you remember telling me the story of how you tricked your sainted mother?"

"I remember," said Fitz. "It was a dry, hot Kansas day when the wind teared my eyes and chafed my skin. I was about eleven, and I ran home from the nearest neighbours, two miles away, and told my mother the Parson was there at the Sonnenberg's, and would be along to our farm as soon as he finished his tea and fruitcake.

"A terrible dirty trick, it was. Poor Mama near had a fit. I'm sure she developed an extra pair of hands as she cleaned and scrubbed the house and us children, all the time cooking a noontime meal that a chef would have been proud of. It was such a simple lie, a teasing lie, but when Mama turned into a whirling dervish of a housekeeper-cook, it became a lie I was afraid to undo. Mama wasn't even very mad when I finally confessed as she was standing on the porch staring into the white afternoon glare, squinting down the road looking for the Parson's buggy.

"'Well,' she said. 'I've done me a week's worth of work in

under two hours. I believe I'll take the rest of the day off.' Which she did. But what has that story got to do with anything?"

"Now, Fitz, do you remember once in Yankee Stadium, about 1935, when you were with the Browns. It was 8–1 for the Yankees late in the game, at least 40,000 fans roaring at every Yankee hit and every Brown error. Two on, two out, and Tony Lazzeri hit a little inning-ending pop-up behind second base. A can of corn. You camped under it; the sky was cloudless, no wind. Yet the ball passed between your hands, hit the bill of your cap, scraped your nose, then bounced over behind first base, while the runners galloped around the bases, and the fans booed the Browns, cheered the Yankees, and rejoiced at your inept play."

"Are you saying the two events are somehow related?"

"You figure it out, Fitz. You've never been slow on the uptake."

"My own sainted mother would do such a thing to me?"

"Only in a game that was already decided. My Maggie says such acts aren't revenge. Just a trick here, a harmless joke there. A little soup down the front of a tuxedo might be a mother evening up the score for a three-year-old puking during a bus trip."

"I don't think I believe you," said Fitz.

"My Maggie says that's the way things are. And you know Maggie wouldn't lie. No one seems to think folk's laugh on the other side."

"If I came out to the lime tree, would I be able to hear Maggie? Would I be able to see her?"

"Well, now, Fitz, I doubt it."

"Then there's no reason for me to believe that it's not your hardening arteries sending you these messages?"

"You believe what you like. But there's something better

coming." McGarrigle moved closer to Fitz, whispering.

"Maggie tells me she's like a scout. She's sizing things up. Seeing if conditions are right. Some night when everything's perfect Mary-Kaye will be there instead of Maggie."

"You really believe that?" said Fitz.

"Even if it's a combination of old age and wishful thinking, I don't want it to end. I've talked to my little girl, Fitz. Tonight I held her hand. And she hugged me and kissed my cheek the way she used to do."

"Can I get in on this good thing? I'd trade any two of my remaining faculties to feel Pegeen's hand in mine, to hear her sweet voice one more time. For one single kiss sweet as a dew-covered rose."

"I don't know," said McGarrigle.

What good would it do me to argue, to push him further, Fitz thought. He patted his old friend on the shoulder and wished him well.

In the deepest part of the night, while McGarrigle was again out by the lime tree, Fitz sat alone by the silent swimming pool, a single light turning a section of the black water a beautiful turquoise. The scent of blooming flowers, of fruit trees, hung in the air.

As he waited, Fitz imagined he had passed back over sixty years in time to a dusky summer evening at a sandlot baseball game. To a moment when the ball hit the sweet spot on his bat and disappeared far beyond the right fielder. He could hear Pegeen's startled cheer, her voice rising above the few fans scattered along the baselines.

As he loped around the bases he caught a whiff of the first essence of dew rising from the evening grass; he knew the game was over and Pegeen would be waiting for him, her sun-blonde hair on her shoulders.

He would walk her home. He could already smell Pegeen's perfume, the sweet and sour of it, and he could feel her in his arms in the shadows of the hedge beside her home, her lips parted for him.

Somewhere a cat yowled, startling Fitz back to the present. He stood and began to make his way slowly down the path toward McGarrigle and the lime tree. His steps were awkward at first, his joints snapping.

Before he even reached the lime tree, he heard gentle noises, and soft scufflings. He recognized the sweet breathless sounds of love, and for just an instant he saw the moonlight-filtered silhouette of the lovers, McGarrigle and Mary-Kaye, beneath the lime tree.

Fitz turned slowly and tottered back toward Lime Tree Courts, his heart full of hope.

The Arbiter

The arbiter has been given an ultimatum. It is his second night home from the baseball wars. It is late October and he has just finished working the World Series, and his wife has informed him he has to choose between umpiring and his family.

The ultimatum was not unexpected. Linda, cool as a loan officer, had presented her case with what seemed to the arbiter complete detachment. The chasm between them had been widening perceptibly for years.

After fifteen years of marriage we are at last able to speak to each other like strangers, the arbiter thought.

"You've got the winter to think it over," Linda said. "When February comes, if you go to spring training, don't come back. I can't stand being a widow for eight months of the year, and I can't stand living with a stranger the other four."

The arbiter knows she means what she says; he understands her anguish.

He was once a guest on a radio talk show in Los Angeles. "Why would anyone want to be a baseball umpire?" a caller had asked.

In the fraction of a second before he began his answer, he had asked himself the same question. Why do I want to be an umpire? Why have I chosen such an occupation? The obvious answer, and the one he began with on the radio show, was, "Because I want to be close to the game. Though it is a secret, and sometimes not so secret fantasy of a good percentage of Americans to be somehow involved in professional baseball," he went on, "there are only the 700-odd players, managers, coaches, and the umpires who actually get to walk onto those playing fields day after day, year after year. Personally, I think it is an honour to be allowed to walk out onto that field, an honour worth whatever sacrifice is required."

When pressed, he would admit that a secondary reason was because he wanted to see the games arbitrated in a fair and conscientious manner. "Baseball games must be judged strictly but fairly. As they say, 'It's a dirty job, but somebody has to do it.'" He laughed lightly, to show the listeners that even umpires have a sense of humour.

What he never admitted in public, and seldom admitted to himself, was that he loved the job because he loved being in charge. More than that even, he loved the rule book. Though he had no interest in matters of religion, he could easily understand how people could be drawn into them, for weren't they based on books that supposedly held all the answers to life's questions? On the baseball field he was in charge, and in the event a situation came up that presented a complicated or never-before-encountered problem, he had only to call time and consult the rule book which would always provide a solution.

Baseball provided an ironclad set of rules to play and live by. Decisions were swift and final, black and white. In baseball umpiring there were no grey areas. Disputes were allowed, but only to a certain extent. If the disputing parties went beyond well-defined boundaries, they could be expelled. If life were only so simple, the arbiter thought.

The talk show host was speaking to him, asking him a question, interrupting his thoughts. How long had his mind been wandering?

"An umpire," he began slowly, not certain he was answering the question that had been posed, "needs a great deal of self-confidence, probably even more than a baseball player. First, an umpire must have enough confidence in his knowledge of the rules of the game to make himself as immune to criticism as it is possible to be. He must also be acutely aware of his limitations, know and understand that he will occasionally make questionable or even incorrect calls. The umpire must remain in charge at all times. A good umpire develops, hones that immunity to criticism, because within himself he knows he is doing as good a job as it is possible to do. At that point the job becomes like any other. Executives in any profession must take the heat, must justify their decisions. The one perk that an umpire has is that he is always right, even when he is wrong."

That was one of the things Linda had said to him, firmly, but without anger. "You cannot be totally inflexible here at home. Me and the kids are not baseball players or coaches disputing one of your calls. At home you're not infallible."

⟟O

The next caller identified herself as a psychologist.

"Perhaps I can shed some light on the motivational factors

133

involved," she said. She named a number of studies she had been involved in, then got to the essence of her argument.

"People who seek to be in positions of absolute authority, such as judges, police, sports officials, have a highly developed sense of right and wrong, a strong sense of order, and a need to fulfill that sense of order. They see the world in simplistic terms of right and wrong, safe or out. To use a baseball analogy, in the course of a season an umpire will call a hundred or more close plays at home plate. Now, it stands to reason that in probably a quarter of those plays a tie exists, the runner and the ball arriving at home plate at the same time. But instead of calling a tie and having a replay, the umpire must decide. Each and every runner must be either safe or out. In the life of an umpire there is no middle ground."

"Is that apt to carry over into the official's personal life?" the host leapt in.

"That could happen," the psychologist said. "But what is more frustrating," she went on, trying, the arbiter thought, to be diplomatic, to spare him any embarrassment, "is when a person with a powerful sense of right and wrong cannot work himself into a position of authority. These are the people we see who become heavily involved in emotional causes, single-issue causes; they may become anti-abortion zealots, tax protesters, religious fanatics."

The young woman talked on, her voice becoming more and more self-satisfied as she educated the masses. The umpire wondered about her motives; what drove her to flaunt her knowledge?

10

The arbiter likes to think he does have a life outside baseball. In that life he has a name, Zack Winters, a wife of fifteen years, Linda, a street address in a middle-sized city in Kansas, three children — two daughters and a son — a dog, a mortgage. Sometimes, when he first returns home, he doesn't respond when he is called Zack, or Daddy. He has been "Hey, Ump," for eight months. Occasionally, a catcher, after the arbiter has taken a particularly hard foul off some part of his body, will say, "You okay, Blue?" Umpires, the arbiter had noted early in his career, were treated like fixtures — the batting cage, the water cooler, the umpire.

10

Zack Winters was single when he decided to become an umpire. He chose the occupation because he wanted to be close to the game he loved, and he knew being an umpire was the only way he would ever get to walk out onto a major league baseball field. He'd played minor league baseball for several years, never rising above Double A. But he'd been careful and smart and the Texas organization had offered him a job managing in Rookie League in Montana. He'd considered his options. As a manager he was afraid he would spend his whole career in the minor leagues. Of course, the same possibility existed for an umpire, but he'd thought his best possibility of making the Bigs was a career in umpiring. His analysis had turned out to be correct.

He'd attended The Harry Wendlestadt School of Umpiring in Florida, established a reputation as being quick and aggressive, learned things he had never noticed as a player. Took to heart Wendlestadt's admonition, "You will be moving." He had never actually noticed that on almost every play the umpires as well as the players were in motion; that just as every player had a job to back up bases or take cutoff throws, so each umpire had to be in a specific position for each possible play.

The arbiter likes the moment when the umpires emerge from under the stands, solemn and silent as shadows. Always just the hint of a hush falls over the spectators as the blue uniforms become visible for the first time, like the silence that falls when a teacher enters a classroom.

They congregate at home plate, the dark witches circling the cauldron. They wait until each manager or his designate emerges from the dugout and makes the long walk toward the assembled authority figures. The managers truly look like boys as they approach; there is a reluctance in their walk, schoolboys moving toward class, a diffidence even in the most experienced, the most truculent, as they extend their lineup cards for inspection.

When the game is about to begin, the arbiter clears his mind. For the next three hours he will try to think of the teams only by colour, the white of the home team, the gray of the visitors.

Some umpires exchange pleasantries with the managers, even a joke or two. He usually does not. The managers make patterns in the dirt as he explains the ground rules of this particular stadium. They don't listen; they know the rules as well as he does.

"You walk like you got a baseball up your ass," the white manager says to the grey manager.

"Fucking piles are killing me." The grey manager grins.

"I'll have George Brett send you a case of Preparation H," the white manager says.

They both laugh. The umpire is not included in their joke.

The arbiter served his apprenticeship: five seasons in the minor leagues, from Rookie League in Florida to Triple A in the American Association; endless games in small ballparks where sometimes the players outnumbered the fans; outfields studded with exotic insects, two dozen walks in a game, twenty hits by each side, and four-hour 17 – 16 ball games.

Then his call to the Bigs. He made his debut on a clear, sweet summer night in Kansas City. He could feel his legs shaking as he took his position on the line behind third base. Halfway through the game, after he had called two close plays at third, and disallowed an appeal that a runner left base too early on a sacrifice fly, the tremors stopped. He felt calm, in control. He knew he belonged, that he would stay in the Bigs for the rest of his career.

The arbiter seldom went out to bars after games, preferring a quiet meal in an out-of-the-way restaurant, sometimes with his colleagues, sometimes alone. But, the night of his debut he went out to celebrate, and he met Linda. At thirty, she was a year younger than him, a social worker in Lawrence, Kansas, about 35 miles west of Kansas City, a survivor of a disastrous teenage marriage. They corresponded the rest of the summer, dated on the two occasions he returned to Kansas City to work. At the end of the season, instead of wintering in Palm Beach, he took an apartment in Lawrence, and asked Linda to marry him.

It is a blustery April in Chicago, the wind off the lake cold as a ghost story. The arbiter wears two suits of long johns under his uniform. The White Sox are in trouble, 1 – 8 for the season. Their manager's job is in jeopardy. Schroeder is at least an acquaintance; they've worked the rubber chicken circuit in the winter, picking up a few bucks as after dinner speakers.

The arbiter would like to see him keep his job; he's a good baseball man.

The umpire is working second base, where he has just heard the rookie second baseman say to the rookie short stop, referring to him, "He's been wearin' a mask longer than the Lone Ranger." He feels old. The White Sox DH triples to centre field. Unfortunately, on the way to third he misses second base, misses it by three feet. Minnesota appeals the play. The arbiter calls the runner out.

Schroeder charges out of the dugout like a dragster. For a second the arbiter is afraid he's not going to stop, that he's going to run him down. But at the last second he applies the binders, leaves five feet of skid marks, winds up nose to nose with the umpire.

"No quarrel with the call, Ump. But I gotta give the fans a show, give the press something to write about," he hollers into the arbiter's face. He can smell cigar smoke on Schroeder's breath. His face is contorted, getting redder by the second.

"Let's give 'em hell," he hollers back, raising his arm in the air to reiterate that the runner was out. "I'm freezing my ass off out here."

"I'm gonna fire that dim-witted son of a bitch back to the minors. I'll send the fucker all the way to Double A to learn how to run the bases," Schroeder yells, dancing in front of the umpire as if he needs to pee in the worst way.

"Good idea," the arbiter bellows, setting his hands on his hips and sticking his face forward. Schroeder bounces like a gamecock, taking a step back then bouncing forward half a step, almost but not quite touching the umpire. "The fans are really getting into it, listen to them howl. You want me to throw you out?" The White Sox fans are standing, cheering Schroeder, booing the arbiter.

"Fuck, yes. It's colder than a dead whore's heart in that dugout. But let me kick dirt on you first."

Schroeder backs the arbiter further into centre field.

"I saw your boy with you before the game," the arbiter hollers. "Handsome kid, doesn't look anything like you. Must have been conceived while you were on the road."

"Oh, now you've hurt my feelings, Zack."

The arbiter backs Schroeder to the infield. All the yelling and walking has actually warmed him up a bit. Schroeder brings his right foot in a wide arc as if it were a scythe, kicking dirt across the arbiter's shoes and pant cuffs.

Now, the umpire backs him toward the pitching mound. He looks down disdainfully at the dust on his trouser legs.

"Have a drink for me. Too bad umpires can't get thrown out of a game on a day like this."

Schroeder is arcing his foot once again, but the arbiter steps back and the dust sprays into the wind, as he gives the eviction signal, turning toward right field as he does so, his back to Schroeder. The manager follows along after him for a few steps, bumps his back with his chest, but gently. The arbiter gives the eviction sign again. The crowd boos wildly. Schroeder throws his cap on the ground and kicks at it, starts slowly for the dugout.

"Thanks, Zack," he snarls over his shoulder. "I'll get to keep this fucking job for another week at least."

10

The last few years the arbiter has noticed that his house does not smell familiar when he arrives home after the season. During the long months of his absence all traces of him have been obliterated. The first days home are more stressful than working Yankee Stadium. It is as if he is a not-entirely-welcome guest, but one who is tolerated because of his expertise as a handyman, catered to because his stay will be short, and life can get back to normal as soon as he is gone. He busies himself making repairs and painting the house.

ı0

The arbiter also remembers what he calls the indoctrination of See Saw Totter. Totter had been appointed interim manager of the Orioles late in the season, coming in from his position as bullpen coach to take the job, so he had no experience arguing with umpires. The arbiter was ready for him.

In the second inning there was a close play at third base, the runner slid delicately, his body an S-shape, his legs like tendrils grasping for the bag. The play could have gone either way for the throw was perfect, the tag hit the runner's ankle just as his foot hit the bag.

"Safe!" called the arbiter.

Totter ran from the dugout and confronted the arbiter on the grass behind third base, where he had moved after the call, anticipating an argument. The third baseman knew the play was close so complained only half-heartedly, generally cursing luck, the fates, the ball, his glove, but not the arbiter.

Totter did not know how to act on the field. As he questioned the call he did a sort of painful jig as if he had fire ants chewing on his calves.

"Why don't you open your fucking eyes," he yelled, his voice quavering with what the arbiter recognized as fear, "that guy was out by a mile."

The arbiter had been backing away as the interim manager approached. Now, he whirled around so he was facing away from the infield, out of sound of the players who stood indifferently waiting for the argument to end, and play to resume.

"Listen, Stumblefuck," were the arbiter's opening words. "Everyone knows the play could have gone either way. You're the visiting team so you don't have to make points with the fans. Your players know you're only going to be around until the end of the season. So what the fuck are you doing out here anyway?"

The manager's jaw dropped; he looked as if he had been kneed in the family jewels.

"Get back to the goddamn dugout and stay there until something important happens," the arbiter said as he turned back to the infield.

The manager was too surprised to do anything but turn in the direction of his dugout. He walked away stiff legged.

"Hey!" shouted the arbiter. Totter glanced balefully over his shoulder. "When you lose an argument with an umpire, you slouch off the field. The manager stared at him in response. "Slouch, goddamn it!" yelled the arbiter. The manager slouched.

ıO

Umpires have to be loners, he knows. Umpires don't even have names. "Hey, Blue," a player will ask, after swinging at a pitch that hit the ground in front of the catcher's mitt, "what was that?"

"A strike," says the arbiter.

"Thanks, Blue."

No fraternization with the players, coaches, or managers during the season. "Keep your distance in the off-season, too," he's been told.

A part of the game, yet not part of it.

"Umpires are lonely 24-hours a day," an old colleague told him the year he broke into the Bigs. "We're professional out-siders, the perpetually shunned."

141

The daytime hours are long and empty: the cloying same-
ness of the hotel rooms, the airports, the restaurants, the
movie theatres. Even the ballparks, the players all blend
together as the years pass. The arbiter is not surprised that
many of his colleagues have eating problems, grow larger
each week as the season progresses; others drink, some collect
lovers, track them like bounty hunters, going from bar to
bar after each game, until they can finally return to their
hotel room with someone, anyone, and not have to face the
deepest part of the night alone.

Umpires are often readers, often self-taught experts in
some field of endeavour. Some are scholars of history, or the
Civil War; some study art, some try their hand at writing,
some are puzzle fanatics, trivia buffs, magicians. Magicians,
masters of illusion, a trade that takes years of solitary practise to perfect.

What almost no one understands is that umpiring is simple. Strike or ball. Safe or out. The umpire is right even
when he is wrong. If ever the old cliché applied — I may not
always be right, but I'm always the boss.

The arbiter has learned to see everything; his eye is
strong, muscled, unyielding — an enforcer's eye. He is on
top of every play; he implores the truth to emerge from the
dust of contradictions.

If life itself were only so simplistic. Baseball is rules. Life is
exceptions to rules. He cannot shut out his other life for
two-thirds of the year, though he would often like to. He
longs to return home in October to find everything exactly
as he left it in March. While he is away he would like his
other life to be frozen in time, for Linda to be as he left her,
for the children not to have grown a half a foot each, to be
something other than large, unruly strangers.

Umpires should never marry, the arbiter thinks. Baseball

players and managers have trouble maintaining relation-
ships, though both groups are well enough paid to have
their families nearby if they desire to. Also, the careers of
baseball players are short; only the toughest last more than
five years. But an umpire's career goes on forever. Except for
a couple of weekends, he is away from spring training until
the World Series. While it is an honour to work the playoffs
and world series, it is also an extra month away from family.

10

On the field, what he hates more than anything are the
intimidators, the few managers and coaches who act like
nasty, spoiled children on every disputed call. They have the
eyes of men who would throw the first punch. The press and
the fans often find such antics colourful; the arbiter finds
them loathsome. They are hot dogs, grandstanders. It is not
as though they are ignorant, or even innocent. They know
as well as anyone that there will be calls that go for them and
calls that go against. If the umpires are competent, as most
of them are, the calls will be fair, and good and bad will balance out in the long run.

But the intimidators know that if they prolong each
episode, make themselves as abhorrent as possible, that the
umpires, being human, will want to avoid the confrontation,
and may, subliminally, when the play is extremely close,
make the call that will avoid the confrontation, the whirl-
wind of malice charging from the dugout, kicking dirt,
screaming obscenities, breathing foul air into the umpire's
face. It is a fact of business that the intimidators, the cor-
rupt, the pushy, the unpleasant, the dishonest, get ahead
faster and further than their pleasant and courteous counterparts. Bastards win. "Nice guys," as the famous intimida-
tor, Leo Durocher said, "finish last."

10

The arbiter wakes in the night, finds himself prowling the house like a burglar. From the bedroom doorway he watches his sleeping wife, a hand tossed carelessly beside her head; she looks to the arbiter as if she is waving goodbye. He checks on his sleeping children. His heart aches with love as a tine of streetlight touches the face of his golden-haired daughter. In daylight she is sullen and monosyllabic when he tries to make conversation. It is clear she resents his presence, considers his winter sojourns an interruption in her life. How different would life be, the arbiter wonders, if he stayed at home, took a job selling automobiles, driving a school bus. Being an umpire does not prepare him for any other occupation. He can see himself as one of those arrogant old security guards, hassling teenagers at a mall entrance, trying to relive a time when he actually had some authority, when he was in control of every situation. There are so many loose ends to family life.

"You can't just throw me out of the game, Daddy," his oldest girl had said to him after he had forbidden her to see a boy he didn't like.

"Life is compromise," Linda had said a thousand times.

The arbiter stands in front of an open closet staring at his impeccable blue suits, three of them, shoulder to shoulder, dreaming of spring. He presses his face against the material hoping for a whiff of ballparks past.

He listens to the tick of snow against the windows, hears the long Kansas wind in the eaves. He has the urge to be on the road again. He has learned to love the travel. While a baseball player has a home team, a stadium where he plays 80 games a season, the umpires are constantly on the road. The arbiter finds a consolation in the preciseness of the hotel rooms, each the same as the last, the same as the next. He longs to have complete control over his life again, over the hotel rooms, over the baseball games.

Pride, the arbiter decided long ago, is what motivates him. Athletes also have pride, but they are able to take satisfaction from winning, while an umpire's satisfaction comes from the ability to bear down at all times. A player can lose concentration, yet be forgiven for his sins — the arbiter recalls relief pitcher Mike Marshall one cold night at the Met in Minneapolis. Bases loaded, the batter hit a sharp one-hopper to Marshall, who, standing as if he had just landed from outer space, gazed dreamily around, not tossing the ball to the waiting catcher whose leg was planted Clydesdale-like on the plate, for the easy force. Eventually, after looking at second and home, Marshall tossed to first, but too late to get the runner. An umpire can never have a lapse like that.

The arbiter recalls a television commercial that admonishes, "Never let them see you sweat." If umpires have a motto, that must be it. At first the arbiter hated the very idea of the instant replay, hated the idea of tens of thousands of screaming fans getting to see his mistakes in slow motion, over and over again. But after the replays had been in service a few weeks he realized that the replays were actually showing the world how good the umpires really were. Time after time, slow motion revealed that the call, made in a split second while all parties, including the umpire, were in full motion, were correct an astounding percentage of the time.

The arbiter takes his pride from doing a good job, for being an umpire means no praise. He recalls when one of his colleagues had suffered a heart attack during a game, he was booed as he was carried from the field. He can count the number of times he has heard the words, "Good call,

Blue," from a player, or manager. An umpire, the arbiter thinks, could go a lifetime making perfect calls and never receive a word of praise, while a hitter or fielder is adored by the fans when he performs well, and even if he has performed badly he has the potential, every time he picks up the bat or glove, to do something spectacular.

Another sleepless night he roams the house, settles in front of the television, plays a tape of the sixth game of the World Series, a game where he worked first base, watching not the aerobatics of the fielders, the balls driven deep to the outfield by the power hitters, but the performances of he and his colleagues. There had been nearly a dozen close plays at first base, including a pickoff play where he had called the runner out, ending a rally, possibly affecting the outcome of the series.

The arbiter smiles as he watches the slow motion replays. He had been right on every play, even though the hometown fans had been infuriated by several of the calls, had booed him at the start of every inning. The tape vindicated him; the diving runner had been picked off, the first baseman's glove tagged his wrist an instant before his fingers had grabbed the bag; the runners he called out were out, their feet still a fraction above the bag when the ball was in the glove; the most controversial call, calling a runner safe at first when he'd made a hook slide, avoiding the tag after an errant throw had pulled the first baseman off the bag, was also vindicated. Even though it looked to the fans that the tag had been made, the video clearly showed the arbiter had been right.

When the first game of spring training begins, the arbiter is in a world within a world. His control is complete, his concentration monumental. As a game progresses, he anticipates every scenario, trusts that his fellow umpires will do the same.

He calls "Play Ball!" and moves in behind the catcher, takes a quick glance to see that his compatriots are in their proper places, that nothing out of the ordinary is on the field or in the foul areas which are in play.

He lowers his hand to signal time in, the batter scrapes away the chalk line at the back of the batter's box and digs in. The catcher crouches, the pitcher goes into his windup and delivers.

"Strike one!" the arbiter calls, raising his right hand. The game is underway. For the next three hours the arbiter is in complete control. Only the playing field exists. The arbiter lives in a place where life is simple and uncomplicated. Strike or ball. Safe or out. *You will be moving.* The pitcher winds again. The arbiter crouches low. Position is everything. Kansas is a universe away, where it deserves to be.

147

Fred Noonan Flying Services

"Courage is the price that life extracts for granting peace. The soul that knows it not knows no release from little things."

— Amelia Earhart

"Empty your pockets," Allison says.

"I'm not positive I want to do this," I say, as Allison gently turns me toward the plane, an antique single-engine from the 1920s I'd guess. While I rest my hands on the side, Allison, like a police officer, parts my feet, and pats me down as if I were under arrest.

She extracts a business card from my shirt pocket, my wallet from one rear pocket, my money clip, bills and change from the other. Then my keys and comb, a pen, Kleenex, and finally, my bank book from my side pockets.

"Today's the day," Allison says.

"We're really going to . . . " I stammer.

"Don't you want to make love with me?" Allison asks, knowing full well the answer.

It's been three days since we've had sex. Allison has had 5 AM calls each morning. Her business is setting up photo shoots. Sometimes she is also the photographer.

I'd do anything for Allison. It is as if she has me under a spell. *Conjured*, my catcher, a Cajun from Bayou Jeune Fille, Louisiana, would say. Her voice, low and sultry, is like mesmerizing music. She is my fantasy. Today, she wears a white sundress with a few slashes of Aztec gold across the breasts and shoulders. Her Titian hair falls in waves down to the middle of her back. Her cool blue eyes are the colour of dawn.

"But, where's my uniform? We're doing a shoot, aren't we? Redbird Flying High. You said that was what it would be called."

I'm babbling. I can't believe this is happening. When she finishes emptying my pockets Allison discards the contents onto the tarmac at our feet. I think of my identification, credit cards, photos. All the years of my life casually tossed away, like ripping apart a stack of calendars.

"I told you whatever was necessary to get you here," she says, her voice a purr. She slips under my wide-spread arms, bobs up in front of me, between me and the plane, locks her arms around my neck, and kisses me feverishly.

Though we've only known each other a short time, I am in love with Allison, magically in love, so much so that my senses seem more acute than I ever remember them. In restaurants I can gaze into Allison's eyes and hear conversations at other tables, smell the tantalizing food odours from nearby plates. Colours have a new intensity. In the on-deck circle I can pick her out in the stands twenty rows behind the Cardinals' dugout, tell at a glance what earrings she is wearing, read the smile on her lips as she watches me, her tongue peeking, massaging her bottom lip as it often does.

Allison works for the Cardinals' public relations firm. We met because early in the baseball year the star players have to pose for photographs that are eventually turned into posters, and given out to fans on various special promotion days during the season. Four Cardinal regulars, being the 3, 4, 5, and 6 hitters in the lineup, the power of the order, were assigned to pose collectively. We met Allison at the ballpark at 9 AM, an unheard of hour for a major league ballplayer to be up and alert, let alone dressed in an immaculate home uniform and ready to have makeup applied.

"I raised me a prize hog when I was in 4-H as a kid," said Foxy Rinehart, our home run hitter, who grew up on a dirt farm near Nevada, Missouri, "and after I washed him, perfumed him, and tied a blue ribbon around his neck, he wasn't no purtier than we are this morning."

Foxy said this as Allison was powdering his forehead and nose. She had already made him apply some lip gloss to his large, pouty sweet potato of a lower lip that was always cracked and sunburned, looking like it was beginning to swell after a recent punch in the mouth.

"Soon as you boys are presentable I'll drive you out past Webster Groves to a big lumberyard; we'll meet the photographer there."

When she came to powder me, I was sitting on one of those blue metal folding chairs that are about as comfortable as ice. She nudged my knees apart and stepped in so close my nose was virtually between her breasts, her perfume overpowering, expensive. I could feel heat radiating from her.

"Got to make you beautiful," she said.

"I'll reward you handsomely if you do," I said. "I'm thirty-one years old and no one's been able to come close so far."

Allison was wearing a rose-coloured blouse. She was close to my age (thirty, I found out later). None of the other players on the shoot had turned twenty-five yet. I had once owned a spice-coloured shirt the same magnificent shades of yellow and red as Allison's hair.

"Maybe we'll settle for rugged," she said. "I'd need putty to fix you up properly, maybe even cement," and she laughed a deep, throaty laugh that was genuine, not the sad little tinkle a lot of women pass off for laughter. Her breasts bobbed in front of my face. She was wearing what I decided to think of as safari pants, khaki with about a dozen pockets on the thighs and below the knees. "Your nose has more pores than a pumice stone, and three bandits could hide behind it the way it's bent over."

"I used to be beautiful," I said, "until my face collided with a second baseman's knee a couple of seasons back. Doc said my nose looked like a zucchini that had been stepped on."

I stared up into Allison's eyes and was surprised to find a clear, almost iridescent blue; I expected hazel or green to match her hair.

We spent the day outdoors at a sawmill, amid the tangy odors of cedar and other cut lumber, the spongy ground layered with sawdust, a lathe operator set up in the foreground, supposedly turning a spoke of white lumber into a bat, while the four of us posed around him in different combinations, looking strong and rugged, some in batting stances, some holding the bat like a rifle, or cradling it like a baby. A sign behind us read CUSTOM LUMBER. There was a photographer, a wisp of a man with the body of a child and a wind-blown fringe of white hair. Allison arranged the poses for him, even snapped a few of the pictures herself.

"I hope you don't mind my saying so," she said directly to me, "but you look as though you're planning to kill worms instead of hit a baseball."

Then she repositioned me and the bat, leaving her hand on mine just an instant too long as she moved the bat up my shoulder. Placing her hands flat on my shoulders she turned me a few degrees to the right; she left her hands there a long time, letting me feel the warmth filter through my uniform.

I scowled, trying to look at her as if she'd just poured a drink in my lap, but I couldn't quite bring it off.

"I've seen a few games in my day," she said. "When I was growing up my dad and I had season tickets in K.C. Name the guy who let George Brett's fly ball drop for a hit so George could beat Hal McRae for the batting title?"

"He played left field for the Twins, and his name started with a Z."

"No points for a partial answer," said Allison, adjusting the angle of the bat, smoothing my uniform.

She hadn't flirted, or acted even vaguely familiar, with the other players. I wasn't surprised at the attention she paid me — I'm used to that kind of thing — but I was a bit worried, for I found myself attracted to her. Many women are captivated by athletes, by famous people in general, often not by the person at all, but by the power they represent.

"Scott," Foxy Rinehart said to me one day, "The opportunities are endless. If a ballplayer on the road sleeps alone, he does so by choice."

I agree.

Wariness was one of the reasons I didn't make a move on Allison.

All athletes, but especially married men, even semi-married men like myself, have to be careful of women who make obvious overtures. Some women collect ballplayers the way boys collect baseball cards. Then there are the lunatic few hoping for a chance to file a paternity suit.

As Allison and I talked over a lunch of sandwiches and soft drinks at the sawmill, the other players never seemed younger to me. They horsed around, like the boys most of them were, talking music and nightclubs, girls and cars. The day was one of my rare off days in St. Louis. After the other players were dropped off, Allison and I went for dinner, where I found myself opening up to her more than I had with anyone in years.

"Ballplayers shouldn't marry," I heard myself saying, "or if they do they shouldn't have kids. Once a baby comes along, the wife doesn't go on the road anymore; another child and she skips spring training. Then, when the oldest goes into kindergarten, the family stays home, wherever that may be, until school is out. That means they can't come to the city where you're playing until July, and if the city is like St. Louis, where the summers are molten, the family stays home in the air-conditioned mansion. Half the guys on the team are in my situation. The season is long and lonely, and absence, as they say, does not make the heart grow fonder. The distances that are at first only miles, become chasms of resentment on both sides. Everyone thinks he can handle the separations, almost none can."

"I know all about separation," said Allison. "I've got a guy, but he's always made it clear his career comes first. He's a foreign correspondent with CBS. Now you see him, now you don't. I'll come home and find him there, he sleeps for 48 hours, we make love, and then he's gone to Bosnia, Lebanon or some other trouble spot for six weeks."

"I didn't even know I felt the things I've just told you," I said. "I feel a little foolish for laying all this on you."

I could tell by the way she looked at me that all I had to do was make the first move. But I didn't. I needed to be certain Allison wasn't a collector, that she was someone who wanted me, not the uniform, the power, the celebrity, the money.

Whatever my wife and I had once had was gone. I'd known it for a couple of years, but didn't want to admit it, even subconsciously. Though we were not legally separated, when I went home to Memphis at the end of last season, we lived separately. I still saw a lot of Sandra and the kids. My phone call home (I still call about three times a week) — a call that at one time produced laughter and I-love-yous, and, from me, a pitch by pitch recount of the plays I'd been involved in that evening, and from Sandra a recounting of her day and the cute things the kids did and said — was, as usual, only a long litany of complaints from Sandra, about the children, the weather, the house.

I listened, saying virtually nothing, wondering how things could have changed so much without either of us being conscious of it.

After I hung up I sighed, reminding myself that I only had two or three years left as a pro. I'll muddle through, I thought. My best years are behind me. I've got to adjust to the inevitable slide, the hanging curve ball that only makes it to the warning track because my timing is off 1/1000 of a second, the step I've lost in the outfield, the lapses of concentration caused by my thinking of my deteriorating abilities. Things will improve when I'm *home for good*, I thought. But the thought of being home for good with a wife who had become a stranger, a family I barely knew, left me depressed, my limbs lead weights, dragging me down.

10

Allison phoned a week later.

"I've arranged for another promotion poster," she said. "One using you alone. Just got the idea last night. I pitched it to the Cardinals this morning and they love it. It will be called REDBIRD FLYING HIGH."

"What does it involve?" I asked. A public relations person once asked several members of the Cardinals, including me, to dress in costumes identical to the team mascot, Fred Bird the Redbird. Another suggested the whole team should be photographed mud wrestling to promote Fan Appreciation Night.

"Oh, nothing to worry about, it will all be done on the tarmac. We'll rent an old biplane, the kind they used to use for stunt flying. We'll stand you out on the wing with your bat. We may put a helmet and goggles on you, I haven't decided. We'll get a big fan and the wind will be blowing the pilot's scarf and my hair. I'm going to sit behind the pilot. After the shoot we'll paint in a background of sky and cloud and ground below. It will look exactly like we're flying at a thousand feet."

I agreed to do the project. We talked on, arranging to meet for dinner after that night's game. That evening I did make the first move.

"For the rest of the night we're going to be the only two people in the world," I said. "No one else exists, family, business, baseball, whatever — all erased. Just us, we can say anything, we can — "

"I know," said Allison. "It's alright to be in love, just for tonight," and she placed her fingers on the back of my neck, and found her way into my arms. I lifted her hair with my left hand, kissed along her neck, nibbled her earlobe.

After long, sweet hours of lovemaking, of enjoying the terrible thrill of being close to someone after being alone for such a long time, we talked dreamily of what it would be like if we never had to open the door and go back into the real world. But the real world intruded on us soon enough, for even though I didn't want to, I began listing the many dissatisfactions of my life.

"I'm tired of baseball," I said. "It used to be my whole life, but I'm past my prime. I play for the money now. I know I'm never going to hit three home runs in a game again, never going to bat in a hundred runs or hit thirty homers. I'm batting .280 but the fans boo me because I'm not the hotshot kid I was seven seasons ago."

Allison leaned over me, her hair trailing across my face; we kissed.

"I'm sorry," I said. "I was the one who was going to be sure we didn't talk this way. I've already whined about my bad marriage and my career. Sometimes I just wish I could disappear."

"What if I told you you could," said Allison, her lips against my cheek, her musical voice a thrill.

"I'm too well known to disappear," I said matter of factly. "No matter where I'd go some eight year old would appear out of the woodwork to ask for an autograph."

"Unless you really disappeared."

"What do you mean?"

"Suppose there was a unique place," said Allison, "a very special somewhere where all the people who vanish without a trace from the face of the earth — a place where they all go to live."

"You're not serious?"

"I believed you had an imagination," said Allison. There was a hint of annoyance in her voice.

"What the heck do you mean?" I drew away from her. I sat up, swung my feet over the side of the bed, sat with my back to her.

"Take it easy," Allison said, reaching out, tentatively touching my shoulder. "There's more going on here than you're aware of."

I recall that and other conversations as I hold the telephone receiver in my hand and dial part of the number. All but the final digit in fact — I wait and wait, then hang up. I feel like a high-school kid dialing for a date, tongue clotted, brain paralyzed with fear. I can almost hear my Cardinal teammates razzing me. I can see the freckled face and fish-like mouth of Foxy Rinehart, who fancies himself a comedian, saying, "Come on, Scotty, how scared can you get dialing long distance information?" Foxy has no idea what's at stake. Baseball and partying are his only interests. He doesn't have an imagination. He has to be constantly entertained: women, drinks, movies, TV, dancing, video games. Allison is right. I have an imagination, something that can be both a curse and a blessing, as I am finding out.

What I've decided to do is, for the first time in my life, believe in something magical. Allison has brought it to me, or at least gifted me with the key to unlock it.

I take a deep breath, imagine myself stepping into the batter's box against Greg Maddux or Steve Avery. I think of the way I let the tension flow out of my body, concentrating so fiercely I can hear my blood circulating as I challenge the pitcher. I'm as good as you are, I think. I've hit you before and I'll hit you again. Burn it in here, across the plate within reach of my bat.

The number I'm calling is information for a town not far from St. Louis. I dial, all the while stifling an urge to hang up at the first ring.

If Allison could see me, I think, as I often do when batting on the road, at that instant when the pitcher releases the ball, that instant when I know the pitch, from my point of view, is perfect, know it will travel toward me in slow motion, almost freezing as it approaches the plate where I will make full contact driving it high and deep toward and beyond the outfield fence. I want Allison to feel the joy an instant like that brings me; I want her to share the rush that completing this seemingly innocuous phone call gives me.

"Information for what city, please?"

"Mexico, Missouri," I reply, my voice shaky.

"Go ahead."

"A number for Fred Noonan Flying Services?" There is a long pause.

"Is that N-o-o-n-a-n?"

"Yes."

"I'm sorry, sir, but that is a silent listing."

"But, it's a business."

"I know that's unusual, but I've double-checked. I'm sorry."

Relief and disappointment mix within me as I hang up. Perhaps Allison, and everything that's happened to me in the past few weeks, is part of an elaborate hoax.

But who would do such a thing? If it were a scheme, it is far too elaborate to be hatched by any of my teammates. Their idea of a joke is to nail someone's cleats to the floor or put Jell-O in a jockstrap.

∞

I recall more of our first night together. Me quizzing Allison.

"Who lives in this place?"

"The truly lost. Those who need a second chance."

"Like the faces on the milk cartons? All those lost children?"

"Some of them, the ones who truly disappeared, the ones who weren't kidnapped by a parent or murdered. The ones who really ran away."

"I suppose everyone there is a descendant of Ambrose Bierce."

"Some of them might be. There are thousands of people there now."

"That's an odd idea. How did you come up with it?"

"I'm special," said Allison. "Didn't you sense I was special?"

"Where is this place and how do we get there?"

"I know a way to get there. There's a company called Fred Noonan Flying Services."

"What makes you believe this place exists?"

"Someone I know went there. Told me how to get the number of Fred Noonan Flying Services."

"Went there?"

"Took nothing with him. Caught a taxi to the airport at 1 AM, gave his wristwatch to a man who was sweeping the floor, and vanished."

"Did you call the number he gave you?"

"I thought about it for a few weeks and one night when things were going badly, both personally and professionally, I did. But information said the listing for Fred Noonan Flying Services was silent. Isn't that strange?"

"Who is Fred Noonan?"

"Do you know the story of Amelia Earhart?"

"Of course. He was Amelia Earhart's navigator. I saw a movie about them. Susan Clark played Amelia Earhart."

"Did you know they flew into yesterday? I went and looked it all up. They flew off from New Guinea on July 3, 1937, for a 3,000-mile flight to Howland Island. But Howland was a day earlier; it was a flight into yesterday. And they were never

159

heard from again."

"And you think they ran away?"

"There were rumours that Amelia Earhart and Fred Noonan were in love, that they found an isolated Pacific island and lived out their lives there. She was a very independent lady. He was tall and handsome, looked a little like Clark Gable, and Amelia was pretty, blonde and boyish with a sensual mouth. Historians tend to think they blundered onto the Japanese doing something sneaky on a small atoll, and the Japanese executed them."

"You don't think so?"

"We're all around you, Scotty. Waiting. Anything is possible. There is a place, a town, a small city really, good climate, relatively isolated. A place where strangers are discouraged from settling, unless of course, they're running away from their past. A place where the police chief files *all* missing person reports in the wastebasket."

"You have a bizarre sense of humour."

"I know."

We were silent for several minutes.

"So, Jimmy Hoffa? Was there a young woman like yourself who was turned on by dangerous men?"

"If he's with us, and I could tell you but I won't, it may be because we needed a union organizer."

"I see."

"Do you?"

"Suppose I want to go. How do I get there?"

"Fred Noonan Flying Services only flies to one destination," said Allison. "People just know. Like birds migrating."

Our eyes met, Allison's smile quizzical, challenging, full of irony. Her pink tongue peeked between scarlet lips.

"I meet some pretty odd people in my line of work," she said.

"Like ballplayers?"

"Sometimes. But there's more. I could name the town where Fred Noonan Flying Services is located. There's a song about Amelia, written and recorded literally hours after she and Fred vanished. Back in the thirties that was how disasters and major public events were dealt with." Allison began to sing, "Happy landings to you Amelia Earhart, farewell first lady of the air."

Until that moment nothing truly extraordinary had ever happened to me. I'd been a successful athlete, I'd led the National League in home runs and RBIs, but I'd never experienced anything otherworldly. As Allison sang I had a vision, and I understood that she did indeed know some unusual people. I saw myself and Allison flying in a very old plane; there was a pilot in leather helmet and goggles. The pilot's scarf snapped in the wind just in front of our faces, Allison's hair flowed behind her; the wind strafed my face making my eyes water. The vision was gone in a tenth of a second.

"Name that town," I said.

Allison scratched around in the bedside table. She wrote the name of a town, on the back of her business card.

"When you reach the operator, you ask for Fred Noonan Flying Services. The rest is up to you."

"I'd want you with me."

"That's the kind of beautiful lie we agreed to tell each other tonight, but just for tonight," Allison said, cuddling down into the bed, resting her head on my chest.

"It's not a lie," I said. "I mean it." Then a thought struck me. "This doesn't have anything to do with the new poster — REDBIRD FLYING HIGH?"

"Well, it does and it doesn't. You have no idea how hard I had to think to come up with the idea. I had to see you again, and I didn't have the nerve just to call and say 'Hey, I know how you, how *we* can disappear forever.'"

"You wanted to tell me that, even before tonight?"

"I knew everything you told me tonight, just by looking at you. I have enough experience to recognize lonely when I see it."

"So, the poster was just an excuse."

"To get us together tonight, yes. The Fred Noonan story has nothing to do with the poster, but everything to do with what we agreed about this evening. We can say anything, do anything. Maybe Fred Noonan Flying Services is my fantasy. Scotty, I can't imagine anything as wonderful as starting all over — a completely fresh start — with you."

"Would there be baseball?" I laughed as soon as I said it. "Baseball must have a greater hold on me than I imagined."

"There would be baseball. But the kind you could enjoy. You could be a star, a big fish in a small pond, or you could coach, or just be a spectator. I can't imagine a small, quiet American city without baseball."

"Could you be happy with someone who wasn't famous? A quiet country boy from Memphis who happens to know a little about holding a bat?"

"Why did you put me off last week? asked Allison. "We could have been together then, without my having to invent the poster."

"I know I must have puzzled you. It has nothing to do with morality. It's just that I never met a woman I thought I'd want to be alone with after we made love. With you it was different. You have no idea how much I wanted to take your hand and say, 'Would I be way out of line if I kissed you?' Of course, I knew the answer without asking the question. I may have appeared oblivious to all the signals and body language, but I wasn't. With you, Allison, I knew that if we made love, I'd never want to leave you, and I wasn't ready to carry that weight just then."

"I understand," said Allison, cuddling closer.

"Are you telling me the truth?"

"What's truth?"

Before I leaned over to turn out the light, I studied the name of the town Allison had given me, and committed it to memory in case in the morning the back of the card was blank.

The next morning I made my first attempt to contact Fred Noonan Flying Services.

Allison and I spent the next four nights together. Then the Cardinal homestand ended. We left for an eight-day road trip. I had plenty of time to mull things over. Even if it was all a beautiful dream, I didn't mind. Suppose I dialed again and the operator told me the number was still silent, I thought. There would always be a lingering hope that the next time I tried I would be put through. Hope, I decided, is all anyone needs. Lack of hope, I decided, was what was wrong with my life.

"I'll be back in St. Louis late Sunday," I said to Allison. "If I get through before then, and I've got a feeling I'm going to — like a day when I look in the mirror and can tell by my reflection that I'm going to get three hits — maybe we can take a little plane ride Monday morning?"

On the third day of the road trip, in Atlanta, I dialed information again, and as I did the same excitement filled me as when I dialed Allison's number, as when I waited to hear her throaty voice, the laugh clear as singing crystal. As the number rang, I breathed deeply, imagined myself in the on-deck circle, a game-deciding at-bat about to occur.

"What do you suppose it will be like . . . this town, this city, this final destination? Can you give me a clue as to where it's located?"

"It may be only a few feet away," Allison had said enigmatically. "Though it may take a half day to get there. It will be peaceful, no more pressure for you to perform on the field or off, for either of us. Tree-lined streets, people working at things they love to do. Everyone will love their job. Merchants will treat their customers like human beings, and customers will act in a civilized manner. There'll be no bureaucrats, reasonable rules that everyone obeys, no alcoholics, petty criminals, no zealots of any kind."

"Did you pick me? I mean personally? I'm beginning to think chance wasn't involved."

"What do you think?."

"Are you real? Where did you come from? Did you just appear out of nowhere in full bloom?"

"I'm as real as you are."

"Which doesn't answer my question. What about . . . over there?"

"I'm more at home over there. There are other dimensions chittering all about us, one or two, perhaps many. It's like when the northern lights envelop you, the static, the eeriness, the half-heard conversations. Have you never heard a whimper when you knew you were alone? Voices in the foliage? The phantom hand that brushes a cheek? The spooky feeling of being watched? Occasionally, one of us is able to invade dreams." Allison stared into my eyes. "I tried. Very hard. I wanted you to dream of me. I wanted you to feel, when you first met me, like we were old friends."

"Have you done this before?"

"We're watching all the time. We always need new blood. I volunteered to find some."

"I don't care for that idea. What am I, a stud service?"

"Oh, don't be so sensitive! Of course you fill a need. Everyone does. The void you fill is my need for a life partner. I decided on you after I made certain you fit all the criteria. If we hadn't hit it off I would have looked elsewhere. But I fell in love with you."

"Was I your first choice?"

"Of course."

"And would you tell me if I wasn't?"

"No."

"And if we hadn't hit it off?"

"Well, there's a very nice playwright in New York. A Bismarck, ND, boy, whose first play was a massive hit, and who hasn't been able to write anything else since. He's sad, frustrated now, not enjoying life."

"What will happen to him now? Will someone else save him?"

"Perhaps. That's not for you to worry about."

There is a metallic clang, like a soft door chime, as a recorded voice spells out the number for Fred Noonan Flying Services. The blood roars in my ears like the ocean as I quickly copy it down, wait for the recorded voice to repeat it so I can be certain I have it right.

I quickly dial the number.

"Fred Noonan Flying Services," says a gravelly voice.

"I'd like to book a flight," I say.

"Right. To where?"

"A special place. I'm told it's the only place you go."

"That's right. We have only one destination."

"Can you tell me where that is?"

"Sorry. It's kind of a mystery tour."

165

"Right."

"How many and from what city?"

"Two," I say. "St. Louis. Monday morning, if that's convenient."

"It's convenient."

"Do you mind if I ask a question?"

"Shoot."

"Why the name?"

"Of the company, you mean? Fred Noonan? No secret. We're dealers in old aircraft, nothing newer than thirty-five years old. We supply planes and pilots to movie companies, TV shows, air shows. And we run these mystery tours, people like to fly back into the past. The early days of aviation hold a lot of mystery. You know we've got a Lockheed Electra, big silver jobby, just like the one Amelia and Fred were flying when they disappeared.

"Fred Noonan was a lot more than Amelia's navigator. He was one of the pioneers of American aviation. Twenty-two years of flying over oceans; he helped establish Pan American Airways; he was one of the first instructors and aerial navigators. Yet he's almost completely forgotten. Ask anybody and they'll tell you Amelia Earhart was alone when she disappeared."

He sounded as I imagined Ernest Hemingway would have, rugged, ruddy, a scuffed bomber jacket, a battered pilot's cap.

"You can't take anything with you. The clothes you're wearing. Pockets empty."

"I understand."

"Good. We get people trying to sneak strange things along. Bags of money, jewellery, pets. There was this banker had ten $5,000 dollar bills in each shoe. One lady had a canary bird hid in her hairdo."

After the conversation with Fred Noonan ended, I sat quietly for a long time. I felt the way I had almost ten years before, when I was first called up to the Cardinals from Louisville: full of anticipation, twitching with excitement. I can see the plane, taxiing down the runway, Fred Noonan at the controls, crouching behind his windscreen. Allison and I behind him. Ascending. One Redbird flying high . . . flying toward yesterday.

🕊

But it isn't that simple. In fact it's ridiculous. The next time I see Allison I try to make light of the whole situation.

"This is all some kind of elaborate joke, right?"

"Do you love me?"

"That's answering a question with a question. But, yes."

"Have you ever heard of *limerance*?"

"No."

"It's a term to do with going out on top. Quitting while you're ahead, leaving the party before the gin runs out. At its most extreme, it involves suicide. A couple like us, in the wild throes of first romance. We know things will never be so perfect. All life's problems are going to wear us down. Your career will end. Maybe we'll have children. Our priorities will change.

"If we died now . . . "

"I don't want to hear any more. Hell, anyone can have a business card made up that says Fred Noonan Flying Services, get a telephone listing — "

"I don't mean die, die. You know that." Allison covered my mouth with hers, her tongue electric, her taste nectar.

🕊

167

"Is it far?" I shout.

"A fair distance, not all in miles," Allison replies.

"Do we have enough fuel?"

"Relax. Lindy flew the Atlantic in a plane this size. Besides, Fred Noonan would never let us run out of fuel."

"Is there really a place where we can start over?"

"Of course."

"Sing to me, Allison."

Her voice is so thrilling, somewhere between sex and sunshine. "Happy landings to you . . ."

The wind, as we whip down the runway, blows Allison's long hair and white scarf back toward me.

"Farewell . . . first lady of the air . . ."

The fringe snaps against my cheek, stinging like a willow switch.

Wavelengths

M e and Brody driving north. We're four days into our trip home; southern Florida to Bellingham, Washington, over 3300 miles, five days if we push it, but neither of us are in the mood to push it. We've just finished our first summer of professional baseball, Brody and me. Neither of us is happy with how it turned out. The baseball was bad, at least for me. Our personal lives were worse.

We chug along in the beat-up Plymouth we shared in high school. I can see a map of the USA in my head, picture our progress, like a coloured bleep inching across the map.

More than anything in the world, I've always wanted to play in the Bigs, and until this summer I always believed I had a great chance. I still believe I have a chance, but my stock is way down. My fielding is okay; I play a mean second base, cover a lot of ground, turn the double play with the best of them, steal a lot of bases if I get on base. Getting on base is my problem. I batted .212, didn't walk as many times

169

as I should have, swung at a lot of sliders in the dirt, and was always out in front of the changeup. As I've found out to my regret, there's a big difference between being a star on a high school team in Washington and being one of twenty-five guys on a Rookie League team, all of whom were stars in high school.

I'm pressing management for an assignment to play winter baseball in Mexico or the Dominican Republic. If they give me the opportunity I'll take batting practice six hours a day. I'll learn to lay off the bad sliders, I will. I'll learn the strike zone, learn to be patient at the plate, practise bunting. I'll lay a towel about twenty feet up the third base line. I'll bunt until I can stop two of three on the towel. I want to play in the Bigs so bad I'll do anything, I will.

Brody hit twenty-seven home runs, batted .276, and was okay in the outfield. The scouts liked his power, his bat speed. There was talk of him going straight through to Triple A after spring training next year.

It's odd the way life works out, isn't it? Brody's never going to play baseball again. He told the organization the day after our final game. After the interview, he gave away his glove to a twelve-year-old boy in the parking lot.

"I'm never going to attend a game again as long as I live, not even watch the World Series on TV," he said, as we made our way to our dusty old Plymouth, which was parked outside the house where we'd rented a basement suite, the back of the car already crammed with our clothes and equipment, Brody's stereo and weights. The long aerial was bowed back, casting a scythe-like shadow across the hood and windshield.

When we get home Brody's going to enrol at Western Washington State University in Bellingham, where he'll study chemistry, get a job teaching high school, and never leave Bellingham except to ski a little up in Snoquolmie Pass, or drive to Seattle for an afternoon at the Pike Street Market. Brody doesn't want any surprises. I can't imagine a life without them.

I feel obligated to report back to my family, but I'll be gone after a couple of weeks, a month at the most. Unlike Brody, I've got a few loose ends to untangle in Florida. If, in a couple of years, I don't advance toward the Bigs the way I feel I should — I've no plans to be a career minor-league player — I'll still head for a big city, Chicago probably, or New York. I want to travel, see everything there is to see, live and work somewhere at the centre of the action.

"This whole summer's been all about growing up," says Brody. "*I grew up this summer*," he's said, about once every hour during the whole trip, whether he's driving, or riding shotgun, or fiddling the radio to keep a fresh station blasting out music at us.

"If growing up involves getting your brains scrambled by a girl, quitting a career that would probably make you famous, would certainly earn you a million dollars, maybe even a million dollars in one year, just to study chemistry, teach at a local high school, and probably marry the girl next door and live a boring life ever after, then I'll stay the way I am, thank you. Not that I haven't got my problems."

"Not that you haven't," says Brody.

Brody is 6' 3" with reddish-blond hair, a wide, ruddy face, and pale blue eyes. He has arms big as furnace pipes, and size XL shirts are taut across his back and shoulders. I'm the opposite, 5' 9", 165 lbs., a bit stoop-shouldered from crouching at second base since I was five years old. I'm dark, with straight black hair, worried brown eyes and a crease between my brows that my summer girlfriend, Mary, thought was sexy, and my mother says she could plant petunias in.

Brody had the grades to go to college, but we both opted to play minor-league baseball as soon as high school was finished. Brody graduated. Me, I studied just enough to stay on the high-school baseball team. If I'm lucky I'll never have to crack a book again, except maybe my bank book. The bulk of my reading consists of checking the morning sports pages to see if I was mentioned in the write-up of yesterday's game.

It was Brody's folks who convinced him to skip college. They figured Brody would get to the Bigs faster that way. We've lived all our lives together, me and Brody, and his folks are the greatest. I remember when we were about six years old, Brody's mom was always the one who picked us up after school and took us to practice, and was right there cheering for us from the stands behind our bench. Oh, sometimes she'd get a little carried away, give the umpire a bad time, or bug the coach too much if Brody wasn't getting the playing time she felt he deserved. But she used to defend me, too. Boy, did I appreciate that. My own parents weren't much interested in my playing baseball. They'd have been prouder of me if I'd been an A student. Mom is a social worker and Dad teaches mathematics at Fairhaven College in Bellingham.

As we travel, the radio stations change every fifty miles or so. Whoever isn't driving has to search until something we like comes in clearly. Until a few minutes ago we had a dandy country music station; George Strait wailed, and Merle Haggard did some songs by Bob Wills and the Texas Playboys. But the station has faded away until it's only a shadow and something else is coming in all scratchy and tinny, some news and talk station. Radio stations can't be on the same wavelength unless they're a long ways apart. A lot like people, I figure.

I wish that just once in my life everybody could be on the

same wavelength. But I guess that's not the way life is. See, if Brody and I could have traded parents, and then this summer, if we could have become involved with different girls . . .

Brody's dad is a huge, shaggy guy who works for the forest service and was away all week planting trees or cutting windbreaks, or whatever. But on the weekends he'd be out at every game, cheering Brody on, giving him an audience to perform for. But Brody never cared. He never tried. He was just so naturally good he was a star anyway. I performed for Brody's folks, and when they praised me it was better than a double chocolate malt, and I'd wriggle around like a pup being petted while they told me how good I was and offered pointers on how I could be even better. Brody never responded to their praise, except maybe to be a bit embarrassed.

Brody's dad was so great. He'd take us out on Saturday and Sunday nights and he'd hit Brody fly balls for a couple of hours. I'd cover the bases, after Brody's dad called out the situation, you know, "Runner going to advance from second to third on a run-scoring sacrifice fly," or "Single to centre with slow runner on second, play at the plate."

All my dad ever had to say was, "Have you done your homework?"

Then Brody would move to first base. "When a great hitting outfielder loses his speed they move him to first," Brody's dad would explain. But Brody complained, almost every time we practised, and sometimes he even acted like he'd rather be someplace else. Brody's dad would hit me grounders for an hour or so, and he'd coach me on playing second base, and Brody on playing first. On the best evenings Brody's mom would come out and play shortstop. She was a pretty fair fielder if the ball was hit right at her, and her being there allowed me to practise turning the double play.

"If you'd just hustle like C. J. here," Brody's dad said I don't know how many times to Brody. But Brody had one speed in the outfield, and that was dead slow. He had instinct though, and because of that he always got a jump on the ball and looked a lot faster than he really was.

While the Langstons sure wished Brody had my hustle, I wished they were my parents. I'm gonna have to spend a lot of time with them in the first week we're home. They're gonna be heartbroken when they find out what Brody's done, if they haven't already. I can't believe that the organization hasn't phoned to tell them Brody's quit professional baseball for good.

I figure three, four seasons at the most and I'll be in the Bigs. I'll send the Langstons free tickets; I'll invite them to be my guests wherever I'm playing. If I was doing what Brody's doing, my parents would be the happiest people in the world. And if Brody had half my desire to play in the Bigs his parents would be in pig heaven.

We made it as far as Atlanta the first night, which was too far to drive in one day, so we took it easier the second day, only drove as far as Nashville. We spent the night touring some of the country bars downtown after we discovered that the Grand Ole Opry was sold out for months in advance. Brody wanted to push on. I think he's actually looking forward to disappointing his parents.

We hit St. Louis in the late afternoon of the third day.

"I've never been to St. Louis before and the one thing I've got to see is Busch Stadium," I said.

"Why bother?" said Brody. "It's just another ballpark." I was parking the car on a dingy street across from the stadium. "It's empty," Brody went on. "I can't see sitting out here at dusk, in a drizzle, just to stare at a goddamned empty ball-park."

"Sit!" I said. "That's the bronze of Stan Musial," and I pointed far across the open area in front of Busch Stadium. "We'll have to get out in order to have a close look at it."

I had this crazy idea that I could still change Brody's mind. A forlorn hope that if he saw the way the light shone down on Musial's statue, casting a heavenly aura around his head, it would be like a visit to Lourdes for a dying Catholic, and Brody would say he was kidding, that the last few days had all been a bad joke. I believed there was a chance he'd laugh that deep, crusty laugh of his and say he was cured of his desire to quit baseball.

Though he accompanied me to inspect the bronze of Stan Musial, Brody didn't change his mind. We were damp and smelled like wet dogs by the time we got back to the car. We set out to find a cheap motel. The inside of the car was stale and smelled of apple cores and empty beer cans.

"So the guy could hit a baseball," Brody said of Musial, and shrugged, as we weaved through an industrial district of St. Louis. No matter how enthusiastic I was about what we'd just seen, Brody's mood stayed dark. We found an eighteen dollar motel, where we parked the car close to the door of our unit so we could hear if anyone was tampering with it. The motel was located in a tampering neighbourhood.

Maybe if the Cardinals had been at home . . . maybe if we'd actually been able to see a game . . .

In Florida there was a bar called Clancy's, a place where a gang of us used to go after a game to relax. Clancy's was a quiet place, too quiet for most of the ballplayers. It had an old oak bar, one wall of booths upholstered in wine-red leather, and a black guy who played the piano, but had the courtesy not to sing.

There were five or six of us who were regulars; we'd pound a few beers, talk baseball, replay the game two or three times. After the baseball talk was exhausted we'd usually go to a nightclub and hope to meet girls. We were hardly ever successful.

It was at Clancy's, though, that we met Sheila-Ann and Mary. They came in together and were about to take stools at the bar, when Sheila-Ann looked our way, grabbed Mary's arm and pulled her over to our booth.

"We saw you guys play tonight," Sheila-Ann said to the group, though her eyes were focused on Brody as she spoke. If anybody had been listening they could have heard my intake of breath when I looked at Sheila-Ann. She wasn't gorgeous, but she was what my fantasies were all about, slim and blonde, her hair frizzed so that with the lights of the bar behind her she looked like an angel. Her brown eyes were deep-set, wise, ironic; her smile was controlled, almost insolent.

Brody, uncomfortable under Sheila-Ann's stare, mumbled his thanks.

"We've been to almost every game," Sheila-Ann went on. She then introduced herself, and Mary, who had remained silent. We invited them to join us. And though it was awkward, the five of us guys squeezed together so one girl could sit at each end of the semi-circular booth. Sheila-Ann sat across from me. Mary sat beside me. And that's the way it was for the rest of the summer: Sheila-Ann across from me, beside Brody, and Mary beside me.

Eventually, the other players left so there was just the four of us in the booth, Sheila-Ann close beside Brody, telling him what a great baseball player he was, snuggling against him, talking right into his mouth. Because I was Brody's friend I stayed, and because some company is better than none, I offered to see Mary home. I hadn't said a dozen words all evening. I'd spent all my time looking at Sheila-Ann, wishing it was me she'd come on to. Mary was a stocky girl, in a grey skirt and maroon-coloured blouse. She had light brown hair and gray eyes

At one point I almost had a vision. I glanced up from my drink to see Sheila-Ann in profile; the orangy light behind her was not kind. As she pulled deeply on her cigarette, her face looked drawn, her eyes hard. For a few seconds I could see how she'd look in twenty years, and I didn't like what I saw. But the vision didn't change my being in love with her. Hell, in twenty years I'd be a retired baseball player, probably nursing a gut and combing my hair forward to hide a bald spot.

We became a steady foursome. Brody and Sheila-Ann, because *she* chose *him*. Mary and I became a couple by default, something I should have run from because it was so unfair to her.

Mary was soft and compliant in my arms in the front seat of the car that first evening. We were parked along the ocean, a row of palms casting moonlight shadows on the white sand, but no matter how she tried to please me I only partially responded. I could sense she felt more strongly about me than I'd ever feel about her.

I didn't appreciate Mary, but there was a reserve outfielder named Becker who did. We called him "Beak" because of the size of his nose. He was a pale, gangly kid with shoelaces of black hair flopping across his forehead, who was never gonna advance beyond Rookie League, and who, that first evening, stared at Mary the way I stared at Sheila-Ann. And as the summer progressed, Becker told me a dozen times how he envied me finding a girl like Mary. Wavelengths.

What I can't understand is why life can't work out a little better. I'd sell my soul if I thought it would get me to the Bigs, I would. And I'll get there, too. Pete Rose was my idol, and like him I'm gonna put out, and put out, and put out. I'll make up with hustle what I lack in ability, and I've got stamina, and I'll practise twice as hard and twice as long as anybody else. I want to make the Show so badly, and I have only marginal ability, while without putting out any real effort Brody could hit thirty home runs every season, make a million dollars a year and be famous. All Brody wants to do is teach chemistry.

10

Sheila-Ann's deliberately setting out to marry a baseball player isn't as self-serving as it seems. She wants to improve herself, and for a girl raised by a single mother in the back streets of a small Florida city, there aren't that many options. Sheila-Ann has the same spark I have. I'm full of a terrible energy and I don't have any idea how to use it except to play professional baseball. That's why I can't consider failing, because if I don't consider it, it won't happen.

"Are you still in love with Sheila-Ann?" Brody asked suddenly, on the second day out. He hadn't said a word for a hundred miles, just sucked on a Bud and fiddled with the radio. The question surprised me, but I tried not to let on.

"Was it that obvious?"

"To me. I don't think Sheila-Ann noticed. And Mary was so in love with you . . . ," he let his voice trail off.

"Yes. I'm still in love with her."

"Don't you see the kind of woman she is?"

"Yes."

Brody shrugged and the silence folded down around us

like a comforter.

◦

Why couldn't Sheila-Ann and I have latched onto each other? Instead, I reluctantly ended up with Mary, and aren't all four of us unhappy. What's more frightening is when I look five years down the line the only one of us I see being happy is Brody, and that's because he's willing to settle for so little. I'll still be walking the blade. If I'm lucky I'll be in the Bigs, playing first-string for a bad team, or backup for a good one — getting in the lineup once a week, hoping the starter slumps or gets injured. Every time I think of Brody, I think how unfair it is when someone won't take advantage of the gift he's been given.

And Sheila-Ann, maybe now that she's been so close to fame and fortune, maybe she will, like an old egg-sucking dog that's had a taste of the forbidden, just keep on prospecting for a big-league ballplayer. But I wonder if she's a good enough judge of talent? Her odds of latching onto a star twice in a row aren't very good. The thing I'd hate most would be seeing her at twenty-five, still sitting in Clancy's, hustling a nineteen-year-old ballplayer who might have a shot at the big time.

I spend a lot of my time fantasizing about Sheila-Ann, about how, when I go back to Florida, I'll go after her, I'll win her respect, and she'll take a chance with me because she and I have the same kind of drive and ambition.

Mary will marry some local who sells insurance, or works with computers, someone who will appreciate her as much as girls like Mary ever get appreciated, and she'll stagnate, and get mousier-looking as time passes, and she'll think of me occasionally, and in her imagination what we had will be a lot more than it ever was. And if she really gets out of touch, she'll name her fourth or fifth kid Charles Jason, after me, and call him C. J. for short.

Brody will get his degree at Western Washington State, and he's already mentioned Dorinda Low, a girl he'd dated occasionally in high school, more than once. Dorinda is a girl who makes my skin crawl every time I think of touching her. She has lustreless black hair, big pores, and eyes that bulge just a bit. She has one of the most passionless mouths I've ever seen on a woman. She lives with her arms folded across her chest and belongs to one of those freaky churches that don't allow women to wear makeup.

$$\text{10}$$

At the end of our first month in Florida Brody's parents flew down and spent their entire two-week holiday with us. They watched us play seven games at home and then went on a seven-game road trip. Florida was the first time either of us had been away from home for any stretch of time.

"You guys jump up on us harder and are more affectionate than the dogs after we've been away a few days," Brody's mom said, as we each took a turn hugging her and swinging her off her feet. She was properly horrified at the basement we lived in so she bought us curtains, cleaned the bathroom, and stocked the shelves and refrigerator with a whole summer's worth of groceries before she left. They treated us both to dinner every night, and at the ballpark we could hear them cheering every time we came to bat or made any kind of a play in the field.

The two letters I had from my folks both discussed how I could make up my high-school credits with evening classes and start college in January.

It was Mr. and Mrs. Langston who landed us a sports

agent and business manager. I'm sure they had to force him to take me in order to get Brody, but it made me feel good. Brody got a sizable bonus for signing, and I got a small one. Brody was always worrying about how to invest his. I just wanted mine to grow a little.

"C. J.'s got the right idea," Mrs. Langston said. "The reason athletes have agents and business managers and contract lawyers is to do your worrying for you. You boys just concentrate on baseball."

We should have. We really should have.

The scariest event of all was the night Brody and Sheila-Ann broke up. It was Brody's idea for the four of us to go to a fancy restaurant after our final game; we both had interviews with the organization scheduled for the next day. I knew something bad was up because Brody had hinted to me several times that he was unhappier than usual playing baseball, but I really had no idea how unhappy he was. I mean he was an All-Star, the press had honeyed him up all summer. They'd even nicknamed him "Bear" because of the deliberate way he played the outfield, and it looked like the nickname was gonna stick.

I felt like a monkey, all dressed up in my only suit and tie. There was dance music after dinner, and the first time I took Mary to the dance floor I spent most of my time watching over her shoulder as Brody and Sheila-Ann settled into a serious conversation.

"Sheila-Ann thinks he's gonna propose," Mary whispered as we danced. There was something so obvious in her voice that I pushed her back from me a few inches, hardly realizing I was doing it.

Brody and Sheila-Ann stopped their conversation and looked uncomfortable when we came back to the table, so as soon as the music started again I steered Mary toward the dance floor.

"What's Brody telling her?" Mary asked.

What I wanted to say was, "He sure as hell ain't propos-
ing," but instead I said, "It may be her telling him something."

"Sheila-Ann was so happy she could have floated over
here tonight," Mary said. "She's planning her wedding . . . "
Mary looked at me in such a way that if I'd been in love with
her, or even thinking about being in love with her, I had an
opening a hundred yards wide to tell her I loved her, or to
go ahead and pop the question. But I remained silent and
the final number in the set seemed to last forever.

"Oh, don't apologize. I don't want to hear it," Sheila-Ann
was saying as we returned to the table. "Just go away and
leave me alone. I don't care what your prospects are outside
baseball. I wasted a whole season!"

Choking with tears she shouted, "I wanted to marry a
baseball player! I wanted to get out of this stinking little
town! I wanted to be somebody."

What she said sounded selfish and bad-tempered, but I
sympathized. And I wasn't entirely unhappy that Brody had
done what he'd done, though I didn't know then exactly
how far he'd gone. I was sad for what Brody was doing to
Sheila-Ann but I was also elated. I wanted Sheila-Ann almost
almost as much as I wanted to play Major League baseball.
Watching the tears splash out of her eyes, watching her face
turn blotchy, her mascara run, I had never loved her more.
There was nothing I wouldn't have done for her at that
moment.

Brody got up and walked slowly out of the restaurant.

I wanted to shout to Sheila-Ann, "Look at me! Look at
me!" I thought those words over and over, trying to make
them pierce Sheila-Ann's unhappiness. "Look at me! *I'm* a

baseball player! I'm going to make it!" But Sheila-Ann stared right through me as if I was perfectly clear glass. It never crossed her mind to consider me.

And that frightened me. Sheila-Ann always had a hungry look about her. I had studied her real close on more than one evening, when she didn't realize I was watching her. She wasn't nearly as pretty as she seemed at first glance. She'd studied all about makeup and how to style her hair to her best advantage, and what colours to wear. Mary told me that Sheila-Ann once went all the way to Tampa to take a three-day course on how to smile and what to do with her hands when she walked.

の

"You know what she said to me?" Brody asks, fiddling with the radio. The tone of his voice makes it clear that *she* refers to Sheila-Ann.

"What?"

"She said she picked me out because I was not only the best player on the team, but because I was gonna end up a superstar. Her and Mary had watched us play fifteen times before they introduced themselves. They planned the meeting with us at Clancy's; they'd followed us there before."

I was surprised Brody had to be told that. I knew it the first time I saw Sheila-Ann smile. Neither Mary nor I ever mentioned the meeting being planned. What good would it have done?

"Seems to me that's the kind of things guys do to girls all the time, follow them around, set up an accidental-on-purpose meeting."

"'What if I'd been a jerk?' I asked her. 'Would you have fallen in love with me anyway? A lot of guys who can hit a baseball a long way or throw a strike to the plate from the right-field corner, have about the same IQ as their equipment bag, and not only are they stupid, they aren't even nice. What if I'd turned out to be one of those?' And you know what she said, C. J.? She looked at me in that insolent way she has, like she was talking to a teacher she didn't like very much, and she said, 'I'd be willing to make certain adjustments.'

"Then she tried to cuddle up to me, tried to move her chair around beside mine, but I wouldn't let her. 'Listen!' she went on. 'I checked you out pretty thorough — I can tell a lot about a guy by the way his teammates treat him. Mary and I, we came into Clancy's two nights running and we sat in the booth behind you, and we followed you home once to see what part of town you lived in. We could tell both of you were smart and nice by the way you talked to your friends.'

"'But what if the only guy on the squad this year who was going to make it to the big time was mean, and ugly, and dumb as a baseball bat?'

"'Then I reckon a man with all those handicaps might need somebody to organize his finances for him,' she said, smiling every inch of the way."

At least Brody had the courage of his convictions. I didn't exactly break off with Mary. I promised I'd write. I promised I'd phone. I knew I was lying as I made each promise, but I couldn't cut myself off from the possibility of seeing Sheila-Ann again. The last night in Florida, Mary and I engaged in some of the saddest lovemaking ever imagined. Mary tried to ingest me, her lips were soft, her tongue wild, she opened herself to me in every way possible, and though my body responded, my heart was somewhere else. To be exact, my heart was in the next bedroom where Sheila-Ann was alone, a Willie Nelson tape crying softly through the thin walls.

10

Before we left Florida, I had an interview with the manager, the Florida-Texas-Louisiana scout for our organization, and a guy from the head office, an accountant type, called a player development officer.

"I want to play winter baseball," I said to them before they could say anything to me. But they didn't give me a yes or a no.

"The computer ranks you 38th among second basemen in professional baseball not on a Major League roster, the player development type said to me.

That was bad. We all knew that.

"The computer can't measure desire," I countered.

"If we took desire into account," said the scout, "there'd be a lot of sixty-year-old men with active imaginations in the Bigs."

"You know what I mean. I'm willing to work. I'll hone the skills I have, develop the ones I lack. I'm gonna make it, if not with this organization, then another one." That raised a couple of eyebrows.

The scout smiled.

"What we'd really like to do," he said, "is give your friend Brody Langston a transfusion of whatever gives you your get-up-and-go."

For a minute I considered trying to make a deal. I suspected what Brody was going to do, and I think they did too. If I could convince Brody to keep playing they'd have to carry me with him every step of the way. I'd be like that goat that keeps the high-strung race horses calm.

I think they were hoping I'd ask for a deal too. But while it might get me up a couple more notches toward the Bigs, it would take the edge off. I know from experience I'd have to earn everything.

When we parted they said they'd call me at home next week about winter ball, and about an assignment for the spring. I think they're going to keep me for at least a year, and that's all I ask. Just a chance to prove myself.

10

"I asked her to marry me, anyway," Brody says out of the blue. We're a few hours from home.

"Who?" I say before I can stop myself.

"Who do you think? I asked her to come back to Bellingham with me. I've got a good solid future. I thought she would. I really did."

"I'm sorry," I stammered. "I had no idea you cared that much."

"I know," said Brody.

10

Whoever isn't driving has to constantly adjust the radio. Stations fade away, become staticky, and have to be replaced by new ones. I'm always pleased when I hit on a new, strong wavelength. But they don't last; it's something about us travelling over the edge of the earth, while radio waves shoot straight ahead.

Me and Brody driving north. Silent. On totally different wavelengths.

Underestimating Lynn Johanssen

"So we beat on, boats against the current, borne cease-lessly into the past."
— F. Scott Fitzgerald, *The Great Gatsby*

1

I underestimated Lynn Johanssen in so many ways. I would have married her. I swear I would have. All I needed was a little time to, as we said in those days — the last of the Sixties — 'get my head together'. At the beginning, I was shocked by having Lynn suddenly alter the direction of my life. It was as if I had been driving along smoothly, and some-one had wrenched the steering wheel from my hand and turned the car in a new and uncharted direction. I needed time to let everything sink in, find some way to tell my par-ents, take whatever shots were coming to me.

I loved Lynn Johanssen. I really did.

But one April Sunday morning, after spending the night with her, I kissed her goodbye at her front door, and never saw her again. She wasn't at school the next day, or the next. When I phoned there was either no answer, or one of her neanderthal brothers answered, "She ain't here." Click.

When I went by her house after school and again in the evening, there was no answer, even though lights were on inside, and I could hear a radio or television blaring behind the thin walls. I knocked, my blows to the scarred front door becoming progressively louder, while a wobbly-legged cur uncurled itself from a nest of rags, and stood on the sloping floor of the porch, baring its fangs at me.

Spring break was to begin Friday, but my dad and I were to leave Wednesday for a ten-day tour of college campuses. Though we lived in Minneapolis, I was getting offers of baseball scholarships from as far away as Florida, Arizona, and California. The trip had been planned for months, scheduled and chaperoned so no NCAA rules would be broken. What could I do? The night before I left, I pushed a note under Lynn's front door, telling her when I'd be back and that I'd call as soon as I returned. "I love you," the note said, "we'll work something out."

My dad and I visited eight campuses over spring break. I got to work out with the best college baseball teams in America; we were taken on tours of campuses, met with academic advisors, were fed at least two steak dinners a day. The Southern and Sun Belt colleges were certainly best suited for baseball, but I was a person who was always thinking, as was my dad, who was a high-ranking airline executive. We both wanted to be certain I had the best education, a degree and profession to fall back on after baseball. I was not totally confident that I had what it took to be a Major League baseball player, and Dad continually reminded me that I was only a strained rotator cuff away from being an ex-athlete.

"You think too much," my high-school baseball coach

often told me. "You're never gonna be a great pitcher until you stop thinking. Pitching is simple. God gave you a strong and supple arm. Throw the ball on the edges of the strike zone so that the son of a bitch with the bat, either misses it, takes a called strike, or hits it to somebody. That's all there is to it. Just do it. Don't fuck around analyzing your curve ball and fine-tuning your slider. Throw your best pitch, high and tight, low and away, paint the black. If you think too much you'll end up working at the creosote plant."

But I had read a lot of pseudo-philosophical writing and most of it impressed my eighteen-year-old sensibilities. Thinking was what differentiated us from the animals. So regardless of what Coach said, I maintained that even minor decisions deserved to be painfully analyzed and thought through.

On the plane ride back from the warm-climate campuses, we decided I would accept a scholarship from Michigan State, even though their baseball program was hindered by the climate. I would study management, graduate ready to leap into the world of business. I knew it was a distinct disadvantage to have to work out in a gymnasium during the winter months, while my competition was luxuriating in the orange-scented humidity of Florida, or the desert heat of Southern California. But I was always thinking, education was forever, baseball skill an ephemeral thing at best.

I wasn't very good company on that trip which should have been the thrill of my young life. It was something Dad commented on several times. "What's the matter, Bobby? You look like you just lost your best friend."

Though I could never let Dad suspect, I was unsure I would ever attend any college.

I spent my time thinking. I wanted to tell Dad about Lynn Johanssen. But how could I tell him I'd be getting married instead of going to college? I imagined his face crumpling at the news he would be a grandfather before the end of the year. He would visibly shrink as his dreams for me withered. I'd tell him when I had to, which I knew would have to be soon after we returned to Minneapolis.

We arrived home late Saturday afternoon. Though I tried desperately, I couldn't contact Lynn that night or all day Sunday. Monday morning, the news was all over school. Lynn Johanssen and my catcher, her former boyfriend, Earl Kortgaard, had been married on Saturday.

2

I never would have met Lynn Johanssen if it hadn't been for school busing. A dozen of us from a wealthy suburb were bused to an inner-city high school. I imagine my dad could have pulled enough strings to keep me at school in the suburbs, but the high school I was being sent to, though in a mean neighbourhood, had the most successful baseball program in the Minneapolis – St. Paul area. Their team seemed to be a contender every year, and had been Metroplex Champion six times in ten years and State Champions twice.

3

I have a twenty-five-year-old daughter I have never seen. Though my love affair with Lynn Johanssen and the resulting baby girl may be the most significant events of my life, this is not a reunion story, the kind you see on TV where the long-estranged father obsessively searches for the child he has never known. The resulting reunion, the tears, the smiling faces, lamentations of joy, are not to be.

My daughter has probably never heard my name. She believes another man is her father. And Earl Kortgaard, my catcher those many years ago, was not the type to marry a pregnant girl, unless he was certain he was the father. Which brings up other considerations . . . considerations I refuse to think about. Unless, of course Earl Kortgaard was as much in love with Lynn Johanssen as I was.

4

"There are plenty of fish in the sea," Lynn said to me. We'd just made scuffling, half-clothed love in the front seat of Dad's car, at the Golden Gopher Drive-in Theater on the outskirts of St. Paul. I had panted something about how much I loved her, and how I had no idea what I would do without her.

I didn't yet know Lynn was pregnant.

"You'd get along without me," Lynn said, exhaling smoke against the windshield. The movie was *Lawrence of Arabia*, one of the most boring movies ever filmed: this guy was riding across the desert on his camel when we started making out, and now, over an hour later, he was still riding the same goddamned camel across the same goddamned desert.

"And it may happen sooner than you think," Lynn went on. "Your parents don't even know I exist. You got something I'll never have, parents who give a fuck. They're not gonna put up with you dating a chick like me. My parents expect me to get knocked up and marry whoever done it."

"If it happens, I'll marry you," I said.

"We'll see. Chicks like me, who mess with guys like you, usually get their hearts broke."

"I love you," I said again, but Lynn was watching the movie.

Could Lynn have been keeping her options open? Was she one step ahead of me all the way? Did she suspect I might not accept my responsibility as quickly or as ardently as she required?

$$\lozenge$$

I never liked Earl Kortgaard, though I was somewhat intimidated by him. He was a hard-muscled, taciturn boy who was suspicious of me because I pitched with finesse and intelligence. Before I arrived they had won championships with a succession of pitchers built like Babe Ruth, who threw unadulterated heat down the middle of the plate and dared the opposition to hit it. Earl was sturdy and raw-boned, with big ears and blond hair in a buzz cut, at a time when long hair was in style. I think he was a little offended that someone as slim and fine-boned as myself could throw the baseball so hard. Earl was a good catcher. We respected each other's ability. We were never friends. I wonder if Earl Kortgaard, regardless of the biological derivations of Lynn Johanssen's child, isn't a better man than I am? That is the kind of thing I spend a lot of time thinking about these days. I still think too much.

Just after New Years, when we were practising in the gym, Earl, scowling as he usually did, when we finished discussing signs, said, "I hear you're going out with Eric and Einer's sister." Didn't even mention her name.

"Yeah." I knew he and Lynn had dated. Was he gonna give me a bad time? Was he jealous?

"Watch out for her," he said, turning away toward the makeshift plate, spitting contemptuously onto the wrinkled carpet we used in place of infield grass. I first took his statement as a warning. Later, I wondered if it wasn't an entreaty to look after her.

Ultimately, it seems my sojourn with Lynn Johanssen has left me with a penchant for disappointment, and an altogether diminished capacity to love.

5

I wonder why I can recall events and conversations that happened to me when I was eighteen, better than I can recall what I did last week? I have lived in the Detroit area ever since I retired from baseball. I am one of a room full of interchangeable vice presidents in charge of financial planning with the Ford Motor Company. My family and I live in a gated community called Grosse Point Farms. My position requires keen analytical skills. I am always thinking. Yet, as I sit in my beautifully panelled office among computers, fax machines, and a bank of telephones, including a direct line to the President of the company, the 1999 projections, and analysis of 1998 sales trends blur and blend like eggs beaten into cookie batter. The reports on my desk are written in computerese, the financial data coded so that only a few of us can understand. My secretary has to remind me of my next meeting; I can't remember what was discussed at my last meeting. But I remember everything about my final year of high school.

6

I met Lynn Johanssen in bookkeeping class. We became acquainted because I have long toes. I knew her name was Carolyn Johanssen, though I'd never spoken to her. She was an eleventh grader who sat to my left, a brown-eyed girl with short, shiny, black hair and freckles, a perfect baby's nose, and a wide, sensual mouth. She spent a lot of time with a another girl named Carolyn, who, like me, bused in from the suburbs.

"We've changed our names," my bus companion said to me. She indicated that the *we* referred to herself and the girl in front of her, the denim-clad Carolyn Johanssen. The teacher was tired that afternoon and placed us in groups to mark each other's homework assignments, the drawing up of a balance sheet.

"Changed to what?" I asked.

"We both hate Carolyn as a name. Since the start of the term, I'm Carly. She's Lynn. It's tough to get the teachers to take us seriously, but they're catching on."

"How about at home?" I asked.

"My mother calls me Carly when Daddy isn't around. 'You'll get over it,' is all he says. He still calls me Carolyn," she said, rolling her eyes.

Lynn had made only a half-hearted attempt to complete her assignment.

"I don't need this shit," she said, laughing. "I don't intend to keep anybody's books. I'll end up working at the creosote plant like my old lady and everybody else I know."

I let her copy my balance sheet, and made a passing attempt to explain the relevance of the assignment, mainly to keep her attention. She was wearing faded jeans, a denim jacket, scuffed ankle-high black boots with silver buckles, the right one turned slightly to one side.

"How about your folks? How do they take to your name change?" I asked Lynn, smiling at her.

"I been 'Hey, you!' for sixteen years. I could change my name to George and nobody at my place would bat an eye. When I was a kid I thought 'Hey, you, bring me a beer,' was my name. My old lady calls me Kid. 'Hey, Kid, how come you never help out around the house?' My brothers call me Bitch, and that's on days when we're gettin' along." She turned toward Carly. "Eric and Einar are dumb as hammers."

Eric and Einar, okay. The Johanssen brothers. I had never connected them with Lynn. They were buddies of my catcher, Earl Kortgaard. Dropouts. Loud, ignorant assholes. The kind of guys who bit the necks off beer bottles. But now I can see the family resemblance, the shiny black hair with its greenish and purplish crow-like tones, the pouty, sensual mouths.

We continued to talk. I eased my shoes off. I had a tender heel on my landing foot, from working out on an improperly built indoor mound. I was a first-string starter in baseball. We were Metroplex Champions last season, I was 5–0, with a solid ERA, on a team that barely produced three runs a game. We were shutout twice in the State Championships.

"You got really weird toes," said Carly, pointing to my socked feet. My collective toes are triangle shaped, my big toes very long, each toe correspondingly shorter.

"What do you mean?" I was a little indignant. "Everyone in my family has the same kind of toes."

"Your second toe's supposed to be longer than the first," said Carly.

"Like hell. Where'd you get that idea?"

"Everybody's second toe is longer, except yours. You're deformed."

"That's crazy."

"You can never be a ballet dancer," said Carly.

I'd seen her carrying ballet shoes. She was lithe and rail-like, straight blonde hair to the middle of her back. "Ballet dancers twirl on their second toe," she added, with a definite air of superiority.

"You're not alone," Lynn Johanssen said to me. "I got the same kind of toes as you."

She pushed up the cuff of her jeans, pulled off her scuffed black boot, the one worn down on the right side, to show off a black-socked foot, the long big toe fully exposed by a large hole.

"Son of a bitch," said Lynn, trying to cover the offending toe. She winked at me. Turning to Carly she said, "Anyway, I got the same toes as Bobby. So there, Miss Ballet Dancer."

"It just proves you're both abnormal," said Carly, but she was laughing as she said it.

"Maybe the abnormals should get together and compare our normal, high quality toes," I said to Lynn, meeting her gaze long enough to make my interest apparent.

I don't think I had ever seen anything so heart-touching as Lynn's bare toe peeking from the ragged sock. I suddenly felt protective toward her.

7

I always felt insubstantial, like a ghost in Lynn's house. Lynn's family were all large, rambunctious, and foul-mouthed. There were generators on the floor of the living room, along with piles of unread throwaway newspapers, beer bottles and motorcycle parts. There was food under the sofa cushions, dust everywhere, chaos. Around them, I felt the way I did around machinery, helpless. Her family reminded me of large, untrained dogs, friendly and destructive at the same time.

Lynn's father roared like a bear when angry. Her brothers, Einar and Eric, fought, engaged in shin-kicking contests, for no reason other than to expend energy. Her whole family launched into verbal tirades at the drop of a word, a sideways glance. Old wounds were slashed open, blood spilled. Forgiveness was implied as soon as the ranting stopped. I couldn't understand or relate to the way they lived. I was an only child. When I or my parents said something, it had been thought out in advance, calculated. We never set out to offend. Disagreements were talked out rationally. Our house, at least three times as large as the Johanssen's, was magazine clean. My mother never held outside employment. If we said something we meant it. I could never forgive the vile things Lynn's family said to one another. Would Lynn, after the bloom wore off our romance, become like them, saying hateful things, expecting me to reciprocate, expecting forgiveness? I couldn't live like that. It worried me. I thought about the situation a lot. I was always thinking.

8

"There's something we should talk about," Lynn said. We were on the raggedy sofa in her living room. It was that period between high school letting out and her family arriving home from work. We were necking, me sitting, Lynn lying back in my arms, her legs stretched out on the sofa. As we kissed, she popped her bra so I could fondle her breasts under the black T-shirt she wore. Lynn loved to thrust her tongue deep in my mouth, a slow steady thrusting.

After a long time she broke the kiss, licked across my cheek, whispered hotly in my ear, "That's as close as you're gonna get to know what it feels like to suck cock. Do you like it?"

"I love it," I whispered back as Lynn's tongue explored my ear. My heart was thrashing like a trapped bird.

"When I suck you," Lynn went on, "when you fill my

197

mouth full, it makes me feel so close to you. I'm close to you, and you're happy, and I'm happy, and nothing else matters."

"I know." I pulled her mouth back to mine. We kissed sweetly, my tongue counting her teeth. Lynn undid the top button of her jeans, took my hand from her breast and placed it firmly inside her jeans. The zipper buzzed softly as I pushed my hand down until I could explore the wetness between her legs. We continued to kiss.

After a moment of pressing my hand between her thighs, feeling her tremble against my fingers, I pulled my hand back, against the protest of her body, broke our kiss slightly and ran my wet fingers across her lips, across my own.

Lynn moaned with passion as she licked my fingers, then kissed me with total abandon, as I placed my hand back between her legs.

It was at this point we usually made our way down the hall to Lynn's bedroom, where we made love, our bodies wet, sliding round and round, our senses full of the sweet tastes and odours of each other.

I was making the first motions to stand and guide Lynn toward the bedroom, our arms about each other's waists, when she spoke.

"There's something we should talk about," she said, her face buried in my neck, her hot tongue fluttering like a butterfly just below my ear.

"What's that?"

"I'm pregnant."

Before I reacted, for whatever incongruous reason, I recalled my buddies on the baseball team joking that the most feared words in the language were not 'You're under arrest,' or 'Guilty as charged,' but 'I'm pregnant.' But then I was always thinking too much.

"I don't mind," I said. I locked my arms around her, held

her tight and close, until I felt my arms begin to tremble. But I did mind. In spite of the fact that I loved Lynn, and I didn't doubt that she loved me, there was some kind of betrayal involved. I mean, I was not careless. I remember the first time we were about to make love, my fumbling through my clothes to find the condom I always carried with me.

"What?" said Lynn.

"Protection," I said.

"I'm on the fucking pill," Lynn said, pulling me toward her, her mouth open and hot. "We can do anything we fucking please."

"So what will we do now?" Lynn asked.

"We'll get married, I guess." The words were thrilling. We'd talked about marriage. I'd dreamed about marriage. But always later, much later. After college. When I was playing professional baseball. I was due to start college in August. I could see myself, like Lynn's father, working at the creosote plant. I thought about having to be around her family: her orangutan brothers, her casually irresponsible parents. I was always thinking.

"We'll get married," I said, this time with more authority, though the words were like ice on my lips, and I hoped the tone hadn't been discernible.

But I underestimated Lynn Johanssen.

"We don't have to," Lynn said. "I want the baby. I've already thought about that. I want your baby." Her eyes were so full of love, everything practical disappeared from my mind.

"You don't have to have anything to do with it," she went on. "I can look after myself."

"I'm responsible," I said. "I'll do what's right.

"Don't be so fucking self-righteous," said Lynn, sitting up, pulling away from me. "You're not responsible for me not having enough money to order my prescription on time. I missed taking the pill for ten days or so. I used my spending money to buy that new pair of jeans you thought were so sexy. I couldn't ask my old lady; she doesn't want to think about me being old enough to fuck, and you know what my old man's like . . . "

"You could have asked me."

"But I didn't. So don't give me this 'I'll do what's right' shit. You'll do what's right, but not necessarily what you want to do."

I felt stymied. I stayed silent a long time. Too long.

"What do you think?" Lynn asked. She moved further away from me; she lit a cigarette, inhaled deeply.

I remember Lynn lighting a cigarette on another occasion. "I'm never gonna quit," she said. "Not because I couldn't, but because I look so goddamn sexy when I smoke. You think I look sexy, don't you?"

"Really sexy." I never smoked, or did drugs, partly because I was an athlete, but partly because I simply had no desire to. I drank a beer occasionally, usually with Lynn.

"You know when I pull the smoke in until it hurts just a little, that's so sexy, it's almost like when you touch between my legs with your tongue."

9

Our first date was to a high-school football game. We walked the dozen blocks from Lynn's house to the playing field.

"How come you don't play football?" Lynn asked.

"Because I play baseball."

"Lots of guys play both. Earl, the guy I used to date, plays

200

both, and basketball, too."

"They say I'm good enough to be a pro at baseball. I don't want to break my pitching arm playing a contact sport I'm not good at."

"Is sex a contact sport?"

"I'm not sure it's a sport. Are there international competitions?"

"I think it's a sport. My parents have other couples over some Saturday nights. After a few drinks they all go in the bedroom and fucking near rock the house off its foundations. I'd guess they're not playing checkers."

Lynn lit a cigarette, took a sip from the paper cup of coffee I'd bought her.

"Jesus, you're blushing. I take it your folks aren't swingers?"

"I didn't even know people did things like that," I admitted.

"A real babe from the ritzy woods. Where I live the only virgins are girls who can outrun their brothers, and sometimes their old man. And I'm not very fast on my feet." Lynn laughed and took a swig from her coffee.

"I see."

"That's a joke, Bobby, for god's sake. You take everything so fucking seriously."

"Sorry," I put my arm around her shoulders, pulling her close.

"Don't worry, I'll teach you anything you don't know." There was a pause. "I'm kidding." She leaned in and kissed me on the cheek.

I don't remember anything about the game, I was too preoccupied with thinking about what was going to happen afterward. I didn't think Lynn Johanssen was kidding.

"We're lucky," Lynn said as we neared her home, "Sis has

a boyfriend with a place of his own. She just drops in once a week for a change of clothes. I used to have to share my room with her."

"I didn't even know you had a sister."

"Greta's three years older than me. I'd end up sleeping on the sofa because I had to get out of our room whenever she had a boyfriend she wanted to get it on with. I sure hope she doesn't break up with this guy. She broke a lot of ground for me. My parents used to raise shit when she brought a guy home for the night, but eventually they stopped hassling her, and by the time I was ready, they'd been worn down. They both work over at the plant."

The plant was Twin City Creosote. Most lives in the district revolved around the plant, which division was hiring, which was laying off.

"Are your parents home?" I asked as she led me across the lawn, leaves crackling under our feet. The stars were golden tacks in a cobalt sky, the air perfumed by burning leaves.

"Looks like it. Though it don't matter. They don't interfere with my life. Eric and Einar aren't home. If they're here there's always some big fucking junker parked sideways on the lawn. It's what, midnight? They're probably puking out the windows of their car. They're fucking barbarians. Even the wildest girls won't go out with them."

Her brothers had started high school with me, but managed to be suspended most of freshman year and dropped out toward spring. They could have been good at sports, but refused to practise. They wore workboots and leather jackets. But, as they say, ladies love outlaws, and at noon hour a covey of girls would flutter about the junker they drove. The braver ones would go for rides, and when they did they often weren't seen for the rest of the afternoon.

"Eric and Einar are just ignorant," Lynn went on. "I used

to travel with them for a while; I dated their friend, Earl Kortgaard. Earl plays baseball, doesn't he?"

"Earl's our catcher. I pitch to him."

"No kidding. Anyway, its no good dating guys who think a fun evening is to drink six beers and throw up. I even got Einar and Eric dates one time. They got all dressed up, but they still acted like fools."

"Was Carly one of the dates?"

We stopped on the listing front porch. Though the house was dark, there was very loud music playing inside, the beat more than the sound seeming to make the porch tingle under our feet.

"No. Carly's just a friend at school. She's never been to my place. I'd be too ashamed to bring her here. I'm ashamed to bring you here, but where else we gonna get some privacy?"

Lynn stood on her tiptoes and kissed me, her mouth open. I leaned back against the porch wall; she pushed herself against me as we kissed, her arm around my neck her fingers locked in the hair at my collar.

"I went to Carly's house once, but it was way too fancy. Her family have a maid. The maid brought us sandwiches and I had a choice of lemonade or any kind of soft drink. It was just like down at the New World Cafe, only Carly's living room didn't stink of grease and french fries.

"Carly's mother was there. She was dressed like a teacher, in a green suit and green shoes, and her hair had been done at a beauty parlor, probably that day.

"Carly's a different person when she's at home. You wouldn't believe. 'Mother, I'd like you to meet my friend Carolyn Johanssen. Carolyn and I study bookkeeping together.'

"'Does your mother know you smoke, dear?' was the first thing her mother said to me.

"'Do you know Carly smokes, and she steals money from your purse?' was what I wanted to say to her. 'And you know that nice boy, Roger, who she dates? Well he brings his daddy's car to school about three days a week, and at noon they drive down by the river and Carly gives him a blow job.'

"'Everybody calls me Lynn,' I said."

When she described Carly's home, she might have been describing mine. We had a maid. My mother's golden hair always looked as if she just stepped out of a beauty parlor.

10

The screen door at Lynn's house creaked and grumbled as Lynn opened it; the music we could hear and feel from the porch slammed against us like something live.

Ahead of us was a long hall, dim, bluish light at the right back. Frenetic music. Radio? Record? The air was close, used, smoky, almost sour. The music was "Hawaiian War Chant", by Billy Vaughan. Shadows flickered into the hallway.

Lynn took my hand. We moved down the hall. Closed door on my left, unoccupied living room on my right. The sickly glow of a black-and-white TV, picture flipping upward. Very old furniture, floor littered. Newspapers? Toys? A bicycle lying on its side?

The house seemed to vibrate. I kicked something, stumbled slightly. The music stopped; the silence was stunning. The shadows still flickered, though other sounds persisted. People had been dancing. The thud of pounding feet took a few seconds to subside.

I felt something like a cat grappling about my ankle.

"What the fuck!" said a deep male voice.

A half giggle, half laugh. A drunken sound. A woman.

The doorway darkened. A big man, a steadying hand on

each doorjamb.

"It's Lynn," said Lynn.

"Fucking record player," said the man.

Now I knew what I'd hit with my foot. I'd unplugged the record player.

"The outlet for the record player is here in the hall," whispered Lynn, holding tightly to my hand. "Only one plug in the kitchen works and it's got about ten things in it."

As I tried to untangle myself, I realized I'd moved the record player — kicked it about three feet down the hall. I heard the needle scrape painfully across a record.

"These are my parents," Lynn said, pulling me into the kitchen behind her. "This is Bob." My eyes were becoming accustomed to the dimness; the only light was from the panel on the electric stove. Corners were dark and crowded. Lumpy piles of dishes lined the counter, overflowed the sink. Plants drooped darkly, unattended.

Her father staggered to a wooden kitchen chair, his knee bumping the insect-legged table, setting it trembling. Lynn had inherited her crow-tinted hair from her father. He had heavy, saw-blade-blue sideburns. Even in the dim light his face had an alcoholic glow about it. She had her mother's round face and brown eyes. At the moment her mother's face was slightly unfocused. As her mother sat down at the table, she picked up a cigarette, one of two resting in a crowded ashtray. She filled her lungs with smoke, exhaled slowly.

"Hello, Bob," her mother said. Her voice was musical, young. Both Lynn's parents were young, in their mid-thirties. My father and mother were both over fifty.

Meeting parents is an ordeal when they're sober. I had no experience being around drunken people. But Lynn obviously had.

She walked to the counter, checked the 12-pack of beer to see how many were still full. Extracted a bottle, used an opener attached to the counter by a string to dislodge the cap.

"Excuse the mess," Lynn's mother said, her speech slightly slurred. "Saturday night we get a little drunk so we can be somebody." She laughed her musical laugh. "That's not really what I meant, but you know . . . " She was very pretty in a dishevelled sort of way. She must have been beautiful when she was young.

I waved my hand to show I understood.

"We'll split this beer, okay?" Lynn said in her mother's direction, not waiting for a reply. "Don't pay any attention," she said, nodding almost imperceptibly toward her parents, as she pulled me into the hall. "They're always boozing it up. They're harmless."

She led me to her room. The music began again, throbbing through the thin walls.

11

"What are you thinking?" Lynn asked. There were the beginnings of tears in her brown eyes. "Do you actually think there's been anyone but you since we started going together? Do you think I'm still fucking around with Earl, with some of my brothers' friends? Do you think that some guy creeps in the window after you get up and sneak off home in the middle of the night? Do you think the baby could be just anybody's?"

I knew the baby was mine. I knew Lynn was true to me. Still, how could she have been so careless? I felt cheated. I couldn't speak.

12

The Sixties certainly weren't all they were cracked up to be. What I was reading about in newspapers and magazines and witnessing on television had no real connection with what was going on in Minneapolis. There was apparently a sexual revolution in progress, something that was more rumour than anything else until I began dating Lynn Johanssen.

In the Midwest young men still got in trouble at certain high schools for having long hair; the wilder kids in high school were rumoured to smoke marijuana. Oh, there were wild-looking kids on the streets downtown, but they weren't anyone we knew; they were like exotic new exhibits at a zoo. I was the most daring member of the baseball team; I let my hair curl abundantly over my collar.

The more adventurous girls were supposedly on the pill, everyone talked a good game, but other than that sexual experimentation was clandestine and inhibited. I wasn't totally inexperienced, but most of my affairs with girls, if such a lofty word could be applied, consisted of furtive groping in the back seats of cars at drive-in theatres, or even more agitated fondling on sofas in darkened living rooms, inhibited by clothes, condoms, and the terror of imminent interruption.

Until I found myself in Lynn Johanssen's bed, sex and thinking had always gone together. With Lynn the thinking stopped and instinct took over.

Lynn announcing she was pregnant didn't come as a great shock in itself. She was so sexy, so sexual. It was as if without even trying she was able to find a series of sexual buttons on my body, buttons that I had no idea even existed.

I remember one golden fall afternoon, we were let out of school at 2 PM We walked off holding hands, hurrying toward Lynn's house and an afternoon of pleasure before her parents came home from the creosote plant, where trees were turned into railroad ties, and the ties were then dipped in a spicy-smelling creosote mixture in order to keep them from rotting.

We walked down the hall to Lynn's bedroom, kissing all the way. I threw myself down on my back on Lynn's unmade bed. Lynn crossed the hall to the kitchen.

"Einar had a six-pack of Coke last night. I'll see if there's any left."

She returned a moment later with a bottle of warm Coke in her hand. She smiled at me, wrinkling her nose. She had unbuttoned the gray-and-pink flannel shirt she was wearing. Setting the Coke on the bedside table she shrugged back the shirt, exposing her soft, speckled breasts.

Since she was standing above me, I reached up, my hands about to close on her back under the loose-hanging shirt, intending to pull her into my arms, but at the last second she stepped back a step.

"Let me show you something," she said. "Bend your knee."

I did.

Lynn braced her knees against the side of the bed. Cupping a breast she bent forward until her nipple rubbed against the rough denim of my jeans. As I watched her nipple darkened and stiffened.

"See, just like you, I got something that stands up when

it's excited."

I reached eagerly for her breast, took the hard nipple between my thumb and forefinger, and brought it to my mouth.

Lynn knelt on the edge of the bed and eased herself dreamily forward as I opened my lips to her breast, my tongue fluttering like a butterfly.

Lynn's left hand was busy opening my jeans.

"Oh, Baby," she whispered. "You suck mine and I'll suck yours."

We rolled around in the tangled, fragrant sheets for most of the afternoon, doing things with our mouths and fingers that until a few weeks ago I had not even fantasized.

"You think I'm sexy, don't you?" Lynn asked.

"You better believe it," I replied.

14

Why didn't I leap at the chance to marry Lynn? Why did I insist on appearing reluctant, on making her wait? The arrogance of being eighteen? It was more than that. My father was a fair man. He would have been annoyed at my carelessness, at the non-thinking that had gone into Lynn becoming pregnant. I know in my heart he would have allowed the marriage. I could have attended college; we could have lived in married quarters. Maybe if I'd had some responsibility I'd have been a better pitcher. If I had pitched the way Lynn and I had enjoyed sex, the clumsiness and anxiety pushed aside allowing instinct to take over, I might well have had a career in baseball.

I remember the thrill of standing on the mound, the sun a gargantuan spotlight illuminating my every move, the air fresh with the odour of freshly cut and watered grass. There was an insurmountable delight in firing the ball to my catcher, watching the puff of dust rise from his mitt with every pitch, until it seemed to form an aura around his head.

Lynn Johanssen never saw me play baseball. She might have been the motivation I needed to stop thinking and follow the advice of my coaches. I would have pitched harder and smarter than I ever imagined in order to impress her.

I wonder what kind of life my daughter has had? Has she been able to rise above her beginnings? By the time Lynn was twenty-five she had my eight-year-old daughter, plus whatever other family she had with Earl Kortgaard. Life is always more questions than answers. I expected my daughter would be named Kelly Anne. That was Lynn's favourite name. We'd talked about naming our children. Patrick for a boy, Kelly Anne for a girl.

Was it Lynn who let me know of the birth? It must have been. No one else knew that I was likely the father, unless she told someone. Who would she tell, Carly? Not likely. Once she quit school she wouldn't have seen Carly again.

By the time the baby was born my father had been promoted and transferred to Atlanta. I have never been back to Minneapolis, even for a visit.

I was at Michigan State when the letter came. Address typed, no return. Inside, a half-inch clipping from the BIRTHS column in a weekly throwaway called *The St. Paul Shopper.*

Dec. 12: KORTGAARD, Earl and Carolyn, a girl, Roberta Louise (Bobby Lou) 6lbs., 9ozs.

Roberta Louise (Bobby Lou) was Lynn's mother's name. Why?

I could see the baby cuddled against Lynn's speckled breasts. I could see Earl holding the baby. Earl Kortgaard had such big hands. Such big hands.

The year my daughter was eleven, I used my position at Ford to run a credit check on Earl Kortgaard. Mill hand at Twin City Creosote, married, three children, wife Carolyn. He rented a house a dozen blocks from where Lynn's family lived when I knew them. He drove a six-year-old pick-up. How I've always wanted to share the good qualities of my life with my daughter, but there is no way.

Over the years I have often fantasized what would have happened if I'd married Lynn. Even now, with my parents dead, I can't imagine going to them and admitting I'd gotten a sixteen-year-old girl — one whose father worked at the creosote plant — pregnant. Bringing Lynn's family into our staid and ordered home would have been like unleashing a family of St. Bernards — things would break in a fury of carelessness and goodwill.

What would I have missed out on? A college education. A mediocre baseball career. I always thought too much as a pitcher. I had the right stuff, but I nibbled too many corners, walked too many batters. I tried to out-think the batters instead of, as a battalion of coaches tried to teach me, firing the ball on the corners and relying on fate.

What if I'd gone to work at the creosote plant? What if we'd rented a one-bedroom suite in someone's basement? Would our passion have gone out one door as our baby came in the other?

I don't think so.

If only I hadn't been so intimidated by my parents. By hers. I could see my parents at Lynn's house, sniffing delicately, wanting to put down a blanket before they sat on the broke-backed sofa, stepping around the loose car parts, declining to eat, even to drink coffee from the scabrous kitchen where roaches scattered like pennies when a light was turned on.

I will always feel guilty for being a coward. There should be a statute of limitations on guilt.

15

"You've never introduced me to your parents," Lynn said. "Never offered. You're ashamed of me, aren't you?"

The answer, no matter how unpalatable, was yes.

"Not ashamed," I lied. "You can't even imagine how different your home is from mine. You'd be uncomfortable there. My parents would make you uncomfortable. I'd be uncomfortable with you there. I'm sorry, but I can't even visualize your parents and my parents in the same room."

"You think yours are so much better?"

"It's not a matter of better. It's a matter of different. My parents are older, they're like the mannequins in clothing-store windows, and just as animated. They're so straight. Can you imagine two people like that in your living room?"

Lynn laughed.

"It's not right," I went on, "but in a situation like that it would be you and your family who would be on guard, who'd be worried they'd be themselves and offend my family." It would be like having dinner at the school principal's house. My parents would always be themselves.

I could only imagine how unhappy Lynn would have been in the spacious but lifeless rooms full of walnut furniture where I lived my life, where I still live my life. My home is not that much different than the one where I grew up.

"We could always leave," said Lynn.

"How do you mean?"

"Take off. Bus it. Hitchhike. I've got a cousin in El Paso, way out in West Texas, the end of the fucking earth. Far enough from Minnesota that we'd only see our families every ten years, if that."

My expression must have given me away.

"Okay, forget it," Lynn said.

"Give me time to think," I said. "That might be the solution."

"Do me one favour?"

I nodded.

"Stay the night. The whole night. None of this getting up and going home. I'll wake you up in the sweetest way I know. In the morning, I'll comb your hair, wash your face in the bathroom. I'll make coffee and we'll drink it at the kitchen table. Then I'll kiss you goodbye just like you were going off to work. Just like we were married."

16

What are the odds that Lynn's marriage lasted? Is she working at the creosote plant? One of those middle-aged women in stretch pants, running to fat, a scarf tied around her hair, who dips her head, lighting a cigarette as she walks out of the gate of the plant, who stops at the Big Eagle, or Bouncers for a few beers on the way home.

What about my daughter? She could have children of her own by now, probably does. If she followed her mother's footsteps she could have an eight-year-old daughter. Or did she inherit my intelligence, my drive, my penchant for analysis and thinking? Is she in college somewhere? Graduated? Entering a master's program.

I believed, incorrectly, that the world was full of Lynn Johanssens waiting to happen to me. I couldn't have been more wrong. It has always surprised me that I have found so little passion in the world. There is nothing so sad as feigned passion. I have been both giver and receiver. I have radar that pinpoints insincere passion.

I did the best I was able to do in the situation, which is all anyone can do. I was eighteen. There were no antecedents. It was like coming in with the bases loaded, no one out, and the opposing team's cleanup hitter glowering from the batter's box. What I did was neither right, nor wrong, but the best I was able to do at the moment. My future, college, a baseball career, loomed ahead of me like the infamous Yellow Brick Road, safe and colourful, banked with flowers, veined with blue, burbling streams.

The choice was mine to make and I made the wrong decision. I couldn't give up that shining road for a sleety-street in midwinter Minneapolis, living like a mole in some wretched rooms, Lynn and a frightening baby as my future.

My biggest disappointment is that my life has been altogether ordinary. Perhaps because I have never been fulfilled in love I don't feel I've fulfilled my promise as a scholar, an athlete, a businessman, a human being. To put it plainly, I haven't done a lot to make the world a better place.

17

After my first year of college baseball at Michigan State ended in May, we were a mediocre sixth in the Big Eight, though I'd had a solid season, 5 – 2 with a 3.18 ERA. I worked the summer for Ford Motor Company in Detroit, a job arranged by my baseball coach.

As a baseball player I continued to be haunted by thinking too much. After I graduated, I spent two years in the minors where I had a mediocre record, two cups of coffee with the Orioles, making the hop from Double A in September, more as an incentive than as a reward for accomplishment. Sadly, I recognized that my future did not lie in professional baseball.

I went to work full-time for Ford in their planning division.

At Ford, I moved right along, earned several quick promotions. At twenty-five, I married Talia, a dark, delicate girl with curly eyelashes. We bought a split-level house in a bedroom community outside Detroit, and had two sons ten months apart.

I knew when I married Talia that she wasn't a very passionate woman, but when she confessed to me after a month of marriage, that she didn't enjoy sex at all, had only pretended passion in order to get me to marry her, I decided my career and family would be enough.

I accepted my lot, lived it out for eight years until, cliché of clichés, I became involved with my secretary at Ford. Talia seemed relieved when I announced I wanted a divorce. She was a wonderful mother; the boys stayed with her.

Ironically, she must have begun feigning passion again, almost immediately, for within six months she was married to a wealthy tool and die manufacturer. I think I've been a good father. My sons are both in high school, brilliant students. We're good friends. They will eventually study at Michigan State. We attend the Spartans' games, three of us dressed in green and white. Has there ever been a day I haven't missed Lynn Johanssen? Even if our marriage had turned out to be impossible, even if it had failed miserably, it would have been better to know. It would have been better to have failed and gotten on with my life. Our best chance would have been to have taken off for El Paso, as Lynn had suggested. Why didn't I have the nerve?

If I couldn't have *the* Lynn Johanssen, I guess I've been searching, unsuccessfully, all these years for *a* Lynn Johanssen. I thought I detected some of Lynn's abandon, some of her spit-in-the-eye of the world attitude, in Gloria, my second wife. Gloria has adapted to become the perfect executive's wife, and somehow I blame her for that. We exist. We get by. We are not happy. What I really blame her for is not being Lynn Johanssen.

18

I actually stumbled on Lynn's wedding reception, though I had no idea at the time what I was witnessing.

On the long plane ride back to Minneapolis Dad and I discussed my situation and decided on Michigan State. The baseball program was good, for a Midwestern school, but the deciding factor was the academic program, where upward of 80% of their scholarship athletes graduated. I wanted a profession to fall back on.

The ten days spent touring college campuses had been like a visit to another planet. The world waiting back in frozen Minneapolis seemed space-miles away. I let myself become seriously involved in the college selection process, even though I had decided, probably before we'd even left on the trip, that I was going to make a permanent commitment to Lynn Johanssen. After that, how understanding my parents were would dictate when or if I would attend college.

We arrived home late Saturday afternoon. I immediately phoned Lynn's house. I couldn't wait to hear her sweet, husky voice on the line. I felt that by now she was certain to have forgiven me. She would be as happy to hear my voice as I would be to hear hers. "I love you," were the first words I planned to say.

Over a two-hour period I phoned six times. No answer.

About suppertime it began to snow, large, soft flakes the size of postage stamps, and in a matter of minutes an inch or more had covered the already slick streets.

"The streets are so dangerous, I'd rather you didn't take the car out tonight," my dad said, after I'd decided to make a personal effort to find Lynn.

What could I say? My dad was always thinking.

I rode the bus downtown. It was snowing harder; I was glad I wasn't driving.

The silent street in front of Lynn's house appeared to have undergone a blue wash. The nearest streetlight was out. The yard, with all its lumpy junk, was softened and blunted by the thick snow. The empty driveway looked as if it were covered in feathers. The ugly clapboard house with its sinister green paint was totally dark. The scene was so empty, the house so forlorn and deserted, I didn't even leave the sidewalk to ring the bell or knock on the front door.

I stared at the house for a few moments, snow carpeting my hair, then walked on. I decided to check the New World Cafe on my way back to the bus line. I'd stop and have a Coke or coffee to kill time, then walk the few blocks back to check the house again. The Johanssens weren't the types who did things together. Some of them would be home before long.

On the way to the New World I had to pass the Scandinavian Center. It was a rust-coloured, basementless frame building that had once served as a community hall, but had been taken over by the Scandinavian Club after the neighbourhood had lost interest in the community league. There was an event in progress. The Scandinavian Center, its front and side doors open, poured molten light across the snowy parking lot. Polka music soared out into the night. Snowflakes turned fiery as they fluttered past the golden windows and doorways.

217

The parking lot was between me and the hall. I stopped, listening to the stomping feet and the accordian-led polka music. I could tell the celebration was a wedding because a couple of large clunkers parked with noses cosying up to the front doors of the hall were decorated with sad, bedraggled rows of blue and pink crepe-paper roses. Beneath the wet snow the roses were rapidly turning to mush.

When Lynn and I marry, will the Johanssens insist on a wedding dance, I wondered? I could see myself, clad in my graduation suit, Lynn standing beside me in a white dress, me trying to reply to the toast to the bride, while the guests at the long, paper-covered tables continually clattered spoons against glasses, an insistent signal for the groom and bride to kiss.

I could see Lynn's huge father, a friendly drunk, roaring like a wild man, hugging everyone in sight, including my pastel-clad mother. I could see my father, cup of punch in hand, trying to be genial, one of the boys, but visibly shrinking away from Lynn's family and their boisterous friends.

My parents would be so embarrassed. I would see to it that they didn't invite my tidy little grandparents to the wedding; they would be mortified.

I walked on.

Was my plan to marry Lynn Johanssen the right thing to do? It was. As soon as I found her I would take her in my arms and promise never to leave her. I pushed on toward the New World, my feet skidding perilously on the icy sidewalks.

AGMV Marquis

MEMBER OF THE SCABRINI GROUP

Quebec, Canada
2000